BE GOOD to YOURSELF

RICH BUHLER

A JANET THOMA BOOK

THOMAS NELSON PUBLISHERS
Nashville

Published in Nashville, Tennessee, by Janet Thoma Books, a division of Thomas Nelson, Inc., Publishers, and distributed in Canada by Word Communications, Ltd., Richmond, British Columbia, and in the United Kingdom by Word (UK), Ltd., Milton Keynes, England.

Library of Congress Cataloging-in-Publication Data

Buhler, Rich.
   Be Good to Yourself originally titled, New choices, new boundaries / Rich Buhler.
      p.   cm.
   "A Janet Thoma book"—T.p. verso.
   ISBN 0-8407-7483-4 CB
   ISBN 0-8407-6787-0 TP
   1. Spiritual life.   2. Emotions—Religious aspects—Christianity.
3. Decision making—Religious aspects—Christianity.   4. Adult
children of dysfunctional families—Religious life.   I. Title.
BV4501.2.B837   1991
158—dc20   90-25671
                                                                    CIP

Printed in the United States of America
1 2 3 4 5 6 7 — 98 97 96 95 94

To
Jerry and Linda
who have nourished me.

Contents

· · · · · · · · · · · · · · · ·

Part Four: Spiritual Nourishment

PART 1

Be
Good
to
Yourself

C H A P T E R 1

· · · · · · · · · · · · ·

The Nourishment
Factor

Claudia was the kind of person who took action.

When several people were injured at a blind intersection in her neighborhood, she lobbied with the city council for a stop sign . . . and got it. When a massive earthquake shook Guatemala, she organized a fund-raising project in her church and stunned the regional supervisor of her denomination by handing him a check for more than $60,000. When it was rumored that her home and the homes of her neighbors had been constructed on a toxic landfill, she investigated the acquisition. When she determined that it was true, she organized a citizens' group that took the matter through several years of protest and court cases with government agencies . . . and won.

I first met Claudia in her role as an activist. She had written me several letters, encouraging me to give visibility on my national syndicated radio talk show, "TableTalk," to various causes from pornography legislation to water rights.

I have to confess that by the time I had talked to her on the telephone several times, including a couple of radio interviews over the phone, I had constructed a stereotypical picture of her in my mind. I imagined her as the kind of person whose house was in disarray with piles of paper and magazines all over the place, whose children were perpetually unkempt, and whose hair was quickly arranged as she went past the hall mirror and out the door.

My first meeting with Claudia was a jolting reminder of how wrong some of our prejudged images of people can be. I expected to be sitting across from a harried person who constantly fought to keep a fidgeting child still in her lap while she showed me reams of paper supporting her cause. Instead I saw a woman who was tastefully dressed, with just the right accessories, carrying an attaché case from which she pulled just the right information. I quickly realized why she had been so effective. Our friendship began that day and continued over the next months.

One warm, summer evening my wife, Linda, and I were invited to Claudia's home to participate in a fund-raising dinner for an issue that Linda and I also considered to be important. When the activities were over and things were winding down, Claudia asked if she and I could talk privately. We adjourned to a den where she invited me to sit in an overstuffed chair.

"I've wanted to talk with you about something for quite a while," she said as she closed the door and seated herself on a couch across from me. "I've listened to your program for several years. At first, I didn't like hearing people talk about how painful their marriages were or how much trouble they were having with their kids. I didn't want to hear about 'bad' things. I kept tuning in, however, almost magnetized by some of the discussions, especially about victimization. As I listened to your conversations with your listeners day after day I began to realize that my childhood was not as perfect as I had always represented it. Somehow I knew that when you described people who had been physically or emotionally or sexually abused, you were describing me. I also resisted buying a copy of your book *Pain and Pretending* because I didn't want to believe that any of it applied to me.

"Then I started having flashbacks," she told me, "especially when listening to your program and hearing some of the candid sharing of other hurting people. I once called the program myself, using a phony name and disguising my voice. After that call I realized that I had been a victim of incest."

The day Claudia called my program, we gave her the name of a counselor in her area whom we recommend for dealing with abuse and victimization. In the months after that, she went through the hard work of getting in touch with memories she wished were not there and seeing herself, her family and the world in a way that was more real.

"I finally confronted my family—and my father—with what had happened," she told me. "My dad denied everything, but later both of my sisters admitted that the same things had happened to them." Claudia stopped as her voice cracked with emotion. Then she continued, "They decided to see counselors after that, and the three of us were able to walk back through those fearful days together."

I knew this had been a season of discovery—of hard work, of pain, of release, and of hope for the future—for Claudia and her sisters, and I told her so.

"I'm still in the process of getting well," Claudia said honestly, "but one of the biggest weights on my shoulders right now is my own family, my husband and my children. I want the destruction to stop with me. I don't want to pass it along to them, and I know I already have to some extent. I guess I'm asking, 'What do I do for them?'"

"I don't have a simple answer to that," I replied. "It will be important for all of the members of your family to have the freedom to feel and to talk and to deal with any hurts.

It may even be helpful for all of you to visit your counselor. I do have an important question to ask, though, which will be a vital part of health for both you and your family."

"What is it?"

"How do you receive nourishment for your life? What helps strengthen you or refresh you?" I asked.

"I'm not sure I know what you mean."

"I'm sure you regularly nourish yourself physically," I replied. "You don't appear to be starving to death!"

"That's the truth!" she laughed.

"What about emotional and spiritual nourishment, however?" I continued. "Do you spend time nourishing yourself in those ways too?"

As Claudia struggled to answer my question, she and I both realized that throughout her life she had chosen very little for herself. As a child she had carried responsibility for her parents' feelings, and she had assumed a lot of the physical care of her sisters. In college she was consumed with achieving good grades. Then, as an adult, she had committed herself to various causes and to providing for her family. All that activity seemed to be necessary and good, but she had never once stopped to think about whether the activity was healthy or whether or not it was taking a physical or emotional toll on her.

Claudia is a good example of many people in our culture, especially those who have come from dysfunctional families. They need to learn how to be nourished persons, not only physically, but emotionally and spiritually as well. Often these people go through counseling where they begin to understand that they need to make new choices and define new boundaries for their relationships. Many, however, have difficulty maintaining these new boundaries and making different choices on their own, just as Claudia did. I frequently suggest they use a helpful approach to decision-making which I call "The Nourishment Factor." It can be a tool for any person who wants to make healthier decisions, both personally and for others.

· · · · · · · · · ·

The Nourishment Factor

When I use the word *nourishment* in this book, I am referring to anything, big or small, physical or nonphysical, lasting or temporal, that adds to our lives. Nourishment is that which provides sustenance to live each day and promotes our growth. Taking a leisurely walk can be nourishing. Buying a new piece of clothing can be nourishing. Falling in love. Visiting with an old friend. Buying an ice cream cone.

For example, almost everyone in the civilized world understands that if you don't eat, or if you don't eat the right foods, you won't be healthy. Physical nourishment is not a mystery to us. Whether we are a member of a poor family trying to boil the last bit of protein off a soup bone, or a millionaire throwing a lavish feast, we know what has to be done to make the best of what we have.

For some of us nutrition has even become a matter of expertise. We know all about cholesterol levels, sodium content, triglycerides, and artificial colorings. Proper nutrition has become an essential part of our lives, which not only affects us but affects those around us as we care for other members of our families or offer our children or friends advice about how to live better. We recommend high fiber foods to one another or the option of avoiding certain meats. This increased knowledge of nutrition and exercise has led our society to be one of the healthiest on record. Yet if we look into the homes that have an exercycle in the family room and wheat germ in the pantry, we see increasing numbers of unhappy people.

I don't need to belabor statistics. Divorce and separated families are becoming a norm. Children and young people find more that is attractive in drugs than they do at home. The number of children who are emotionally, physically, and sexually abused is alarming, and the number of adults finally recognizing the effects of abuse in their own childhood years has produced huge markets for books, seminars, and self-help programs. Even many Christians, who have long believed that their faith would produce a better life for them than the non-Christian next door, are finding themselves sitting in the same counseling offices with the same questions as everyone else.

Nourishment can be visible and material, or it can be invisible and emotional or spiritual. Visible nourishment is temporary. Invisible nourishment is much deeper than the material world and can have eternal significance.

Invisible Nourishment

Even though we have become experts in physical nourishment, we are astonishingly ignorant about that which nourishes us at a deeper level. To use a biblical metaphor, the "outer man" looks very impressive and well nourished; the "inner man," however, is famished. If we were able to take photographs of this inner man, we would see people with sunken eyes and protruding bones, dragging themselves through the streets with the same look of hopelessness as victims of a drought.

What has contributed to this condition? How have we developed a society with the finest possessions and some of the richest opportunities in recorded history, and yet a society that is starving emotionally and spiritually? One factor has been that our culture has been preoccupied by that which is material and visible and has not given as much value to that which is invisible. The visible world consists of homes and cars and businesses and money. The invisible world consists of love and integrity and God and eternity.

The average person spends more time accumulating

things than serving God because things are more real. In fact, until recent years, the supernatural, which is essentially a part of the invisible world, has not had much modern acceptance. The result has been that wonderful people who have a genuine desire to live a good life have committed themselves faithfully to that which is visible at the expense of that which is invisible.

A recent study, for example, showed that many women who thought it was going to be most fulfilling to forsake marriage and children in favor of a career (or who delegated the rearing of their children to others) have concluded, after twenty years, that it was a mistake.

God has constructed human beings with a natural need to be nourished. Yet the word *nourishment* has almost no practical meaning for some of us. It has been years since we made even a tiny choice that could be called nourishing. Even when it comes to eating, many of us are grabbing a quick mouthful of junk food while we rush from one engagement to another. If we lack nourishment, we will know it by the ache and the longing that is in our bodies and our hearts and our spirits.

That longing is called hunger.

Hunger

Most of us understand how driven a hungry person can be. Yet, in many of our cultures we have never really known extended physical hunger. We sometimes describe ourselves as "famished" or "starved," but that usually means that it's been three or four hours since our last hamburger. Few of us have really ever experienced true physical starvation. Even so, each of us probably has had some experience of intense hunger, which helps us personally identify how powerful hunger can be.

The first signs of hunger may be easy to ignore and most of us can delay responding until we finish whatever we're doing or until the next meal is scheduled to be served.

Once the hunger builds, however, we become committed to satisfying it and ultimately become consumed by this desire. Try to imagine a person who has not had anything to eat for a week sitting through a business conference without being distracted if doughnuts or hors d'oeuvres or something else to eat is on the table. When we get hungry enough, other interests or concerns or responsibilities will be set aside until the hunger is somehow addressed. Desperately hungry people have allowed themselves to do things they would never have done otherwise.

Today many of us are making choices to respond to this desperate hunger. We have not been able to pay attention to our jobs or our families as we should because life consists of daily climbing out of bed and seeking whatever emotional and spiritual morsels we can find. What makes this additionally pitiful is that most of us are trying to pretend that we are not hungry. We associate various kinds of hunger with failure and ineligibility.

Perhaps we were reared in homes where we were not allowed to express our hunger because it made others feel uncomfortable or suggested that they were failures. That attitude also existed outside our homes at school or among family or at church. To be hungry was not a sign of success; to admit hunger made people feel uncomfortable. We dressed our emaciated souls and spirits in clothes designed to hide the hunger and walked among our friends and relatives trying to appear well-nourished when we were preoccupied with the ache inside.

Many of us, like Claudia, need to make new choices for ourselves and our families.

· · · · · · · · ·
New Choices

Claudia was a person who needed to make quite a few new choices that would lead to nourishment for herself and her family.

"You'll have to deal with this in more depth in the next several weeks," I told her, "but, just for sake of discussion, think of a choice you could make in the next day or two that would be nourishing to you."

The long silence that followed my challenge was as revealing as the discussion that came next. As Claudia talked about some of her options, she sounded as if she were trying to make a decision for someone else and was having difficulty knowing what that other person might enjoy. There was no passion, no conviction. She numbly went through a list of what she had seen other people do to provide nourishment in their lives, such as golfing or traveling or reading. But the tone of her voice told me that she didn't have any interest in any of these activities.

"I know that many people enjoy volunteer activities," she finally said, "but I. . . ." The sentence was never completed, but we both knew the ending.

Reluctantly Claudia admitted that although some of her successes had meant a lot to her, much of her volunteer activity had been driven by her desire for other people's approval.

She then realized that even some of the activities in her life that had the appearance of emotional and spiritual nourishment were not very satisfying to her. She accepted social engagements largely because she felt she "had to go." Church had become an obligation. Before the evening was over, Claudia came to the jarring conclusion that virtually none of the choices she had made as an adult had been very nourishing to her.

Claudia eventually decided that one of the first steps she needed to take to add nourishment to her life was to arrange to have lunch at least three or four times a month with a dear friend of hers. "I'm always nourished by being with her," Claudia told me. "We have been very close friends for many years, and there have been times we have been important sources of support for each other. But those times, I realize, have been mostly during huge crises. We shouldn't have to wait for the bottom to drop out to be nourished by one another."

Claudia's decision to get together with her friend was important because it was one of the first choices she had made in a long time that was designed to contribute to her own nourishment, even in a small way. This choice wouldn't change the course of her life, but it was an initial response to her empty feeling.

Claudia also needed to evaluate the boundaries between herself and other people. Claudia threw herself into every person's life who had a need or who made a request of her. She discovered that it was difficult to say "no." She had never decided where her boundaries should be or thought about how she could enforce them.

· · · · · · · · ·

New Boundaries

When I think of a boundary, I think of something that distinguishes between one territory and another, like the border between Canada and the United States. The border makes it clear that I am leaving my territory and entering another territory.

Sometimes people from both sides of a boundary freely cross over into one another's territory, presumably for one another's benefit. Other times a boundary is a protective barrier that keeps people safe, like the Alps, which have historically kept the Swiss from being invaded. Sometimes a country's border needs to be protected. The Nourishment Factor can help us define boundaries and, when necessary, help us protect them. It can also help us see and respect other people's boundaries.

On the face of it, there was nothing wrong with Claudia's volunteer activities. She was nourishing a lot of people. But when she came to realize that she was virtually ignoring her own nourishment and, therefore, her ability to continue nourishing others, she had to draw the line.

She needed to learn to say, "Not this time." Previously she had set the boundary whenever she either became exhausted or got fed up or when her family insisted that she was doing too much. Now she could ask herself the question, "Am I basically a nourished person? If so, I can probably launch out and do things to help other people. If not, I cannot afford to endanger my routine nourishment by saying 'yes' to too many things."

Let me say emphatically at the end of this chapter that I am not suggesting we should devalue or despise visible nourishment. Some people mistakenly believe that since invisible nourishment is deeper and more eternal, our lives should be exclusively committed to the invisible. I'll have more to say about that in a later chapter but, ultimately, that attitude does not nourish. God intends for us to experience nourishment at all levels—physical, emotional, and spiritual; to deprecate the physical is to rob ourselves of much of the richness of life. On the other hand, to focus on the physical and to make that the most important consideration is not good either. In reality, life will consist of wonderful moments of physical, visible nourishment, which have little meaning except for the moment they occur, as well as moments of emotional and spiritual nourishment, which will never be forgotten.

Enjoying a good meal, for example, is a physical, visible experience. Yet a meal can also include invisible significance. Imagine a cozy dinner for two, which is emotionally nourishing to the husband and wife who are sharing it together. Think of the central meal of a family reunion. The memory that will last is the experience of people who love one another and may not have been together for quite a while enjoying one another's company. Or picture the father and his son on a hunting trip who are cooking their evening meal over an open fire and creating memories that will last a lifetime. Sometimes both the visible and the invisible can occur at the same time.

I have divided this book into four parts. In Part Two we will look at the ABCs of nourishment—the elementary principles that help us to make healthy new choices and establish new boundaries. The process will seem so simple and easy to apply that you will wonder, Why don't we make these decisions naturally? I'll answer that question at the end of Part Two. Unfortunately roadblocks occur along the way to these healthy choices. Once we recognize them and learn some techniques to avoid feelings like guilt and fear, we'll be able to make these new choices more naturally.

Then in Part Three we will talk about nourishing others, our friends, our spouses, and our children. Specific principles of nourishment apply to these special people. Finally in Part Four we will look at spiritual nourishment, an essential aspect of every person's life.

Is your life full and joyful? Is your marriage well nourished? Do you have nourishing relationships with your children or with God? If not, consider The Nourishment Factor. This simple, natural way to make decisions changed Claudia's life. It will change yours too.

P A R T   2

The ABCs of Nourishment

CHAPTER 2

. . . .

Nourishment
Begins
with Yourself

Perry, a business friend of mine with whom I have lunch from time to time, owns his own public relations firm and has been modestly successful. He's also a workaholic and brags about it. His wife once told me, "I gave up trying to make him slow down a long time ago. Instead I decided to construct a life of my own outside of his break-neck world."

Perry's pace was brought to a shattering halt by a heart attack, which nearly killed him. For the first time he listened to a doctor's warning that his life-style needed to change. During one of our lunches after his heart attack, I brought up the subject of emotional and spiritual nourishment, and we discussed it at length.

Not surprisingly, Perry had already come to realize that he didn't make enough personally nourishing choices, but the thought of doing so troubled him. "I was taught by my parents and my church that joy was going to be found by putting myself last," he told me. "In fact, the word *joy* meant, 'Jesus, others, and you.' In that order. It just seems selfish if I take time for myself."

"It isn't fulfilling or very Christian to live only for yourself and your own needs," I replied. "Christ taught us to be different from some of the religious leaders of his day who ignored the needy and the hurting. That's what the story of the good Samaritan is all about: a man who was willing to interrupt his schedule and use his wealth to help a victim he found along the road, even though that victim was from among a group of people that the Samaritans traditionally despised. It is important for us to offer our lives to God and to others as a matter of commitment. But in order to fulfill that commitment, we've got to be nourished! That's a basic minimum. I don't think God gives us an assignment of service and expects us to disregard the nourishment we need to accomplish it."

· · · · · · · · ·
We Need Nourishment in Order to Serve

Perry's fears are representative of the feelings many of us have. I've had to struggle with the guilt that I'm being self-centered when I pay attention to my own needs. The fact remains, however, that the first step toward living a nourishing life, and even committing ourselves to the nourishment of others, is to pay attention to our own basic nourishment. That's not selfish. It's sensible. And it's only the beginning.

What is your mission in life? Is it to serve God in some unique way? Is it to minister to your spouse or your family or your neighbors? Is it to rescue the victims or to heal the wounded? Is it to make the world a better place to live?

You will not do any of those things very effectively without making choices for the nourishment of your own life. Hungry people cannot work as effectively as those whose needs for nourishment have been satisfied.

I told that to Perry. Then I suggested, "Let's imagine you are sent to a part of the world where there is famine and that your mission is to feed those who are hungry. Starving people are going to rely on you for their sustenance. Let's also imagine that when you get there, you feel so guilty about their need that you just can't bring yourself to eat any meals of your own. You skip breakfast, lunch, and dinner, and work tirelessly to feed the people; you even give your own rations away. That sounds selfless and caring on the surface. But it is irresponsible—not only for yourself but for those people as well.

"It will be only a matter of days before you will not be able to adequately serve the very people you allegedly committed yourself to nourish. It will be a matter of weeks before you could actually die because of all your selfless giving. While it would have been selfish, perhaps, to stay at home and devote yourself to your own nourishment, it is not selfish for you to pay attention to your own needs as you serve and nourish others. In fact, it is a part of your commitment to them. You must take time to eat your own meals. You must take time for personal and spiritual refreshment. You must take time to be alone. Otherwise you will either fail to nourish them properly or eventually burn out trying to nourish them at all."

"I guess I just can't imagine Jesus taking time off from all the people who needed him," Perry responded.

"You can't? Think of all the times Jesus slipped away from the crowds demanding his attention in order to be in quiet places where he could receive emotional and spiritual nourishment. He and his disciples would travel from hot, dusty Jerusalem to the beauty and the green hills of Galilee to 'a quiet place to rest' for a while. There is no evidence that Jesus neglected that which fed both his body and his spirit as a part of his commitment to the people. To the contrary. He was a hungry person—hungry for food, hungry for friends and co-workers, hungry to do the will of God. He did not ignore any of those hungers even though he did not selfishly live just to satisfy his own needs."

"I've never thought about it before," Perry responded. "But as you were talking about Jesus, I realize that the Good Samaritan must have been paying attention to his own basic needs or else he wouldn't have had the money to pay for the lodging and medical care of the man he found along the road."

"Now you're getting the picture."

One of my favorite quotes about nourishment comes from a friend of mine, author/speaker Joyce Penner. One day she and her husband, Cliff, and I got to talking about the importance of personal nourishment.

"Oh, that's one of my favorite topics," Joyce said, looking at Cliff with a twinkle in her eye. It was as though she were saying, "You need to think about it more often, Dear!"

"I usually take an afternoon nap," she told me. "That's when I tell the children they are on their own for a while, and I need to be by myself. I consider that nap to be a gift to my family."

I love that. Her nap meant that her children and husband were going to enjoy a refreshed, energetic, happy mother. The same could be said for any commitment in our lives. For us to be nourished personally is a gift to our families, our friends, our employers, and our God.

If You Haven't Been Nourished, You Cannot Nourish Others

There's another important reason for paying attention to your own basic nourishment: your experiences in nourishing yourself will help you know how to nourish others.

It is folly to try to talk other people into living nourished lives when we don't even know what that is! How would you like your physical nourishment to be in the hands of a person who has never personally experienced it? Can you imagine what those meals would taste like? Can you imagine what the ingredients might be? We draw from our own experience in order to help others. We imagine what they need and what will "taste" good, or will be truly nutritious, based on our own experience with food.

The Woman Whose Taste Was Twisted

While in college, I sang with a quartet that toured the United States each summer representing our school. The members of the quartet were all good friends, and we had some wonderful times singing at various churches and camps and meeting all kinds of people.

One of our most memorable experiences occurred in a small town in Colorado. We had been invited to perform for a struggling church that had a part-time pastor and met in the basement of a retail shop. As was the custom, we were all invited to the home of one of the members to refresh ourselves before the meeting and to have dinner.

We knew we were in trouble as soon as we walked through the door. Years of cobwebs hung from the ceilings. Massive collections of magazines leaned against the walls. It looked as if we had stumbled across the notorious TV family "The Munsters."

The woman of the house was a precious and sincere lady, but she had obviously come from a tragically dysfunctional family and was carrying on the tradition. The children were dirty and smelly. The bathrooms in the house hadn't been cleaned in years and seemed to house an array of biological accidents and experiments. None of us could bring ourselves to use the bathroom for *anything*. I remember the look on the face of the only woman in our group, the wife of one of the quartet members, as we toured the house. Her expression clearly said, "I don't want to be here."

The real adventure, however, was dinner. By this time

the hunger that we had spent the afternoon developing had died an unnatural death. As we sat down, our hostess pulled an enormous turkey out of the oven and set it in the middle of the table.

Even as a college student who had never cooked a Thanksgiving dinner, I thought to myself, *I'm no expert on cooking turkeys, but this one does not look like it's done.*

After leading us in grace, the woman ceremoniously began carving the main course. As each slice fell into the goo at the bottom of the pan it was agonizingly clear that the heat had penetrated only an inch of the bird and the rest of it was as raw as when it came from the butcher! The flustered woman muttered something about having "left the turkey in the oven for a whole hour." Her experience at preparing meals probably had been limited to pouring milk over Cheerios.

After a moment of silence, in which the woman realized she didn't have time to cook the turkey for another three or four hours, since we had to be at the church in an hour-and-a-half, she decided to fry the turkey slices in bacon grease of unknown age.

Once that was accomplished, the woman began passing the plate of turkey slices and bowls of potatoes and vegetables around the table. I watched in amazement as her children used their hands to scoop gobs of cold beans from the serving bowl onto their plates. Not too long after that, a two-gallon container of iced tea burst because it wasn't strong enough to handle the load. I think the container was meant for holding flowers!

This dear woman had virtually nothing to offer us that was strengthening or appealing. Her heart was right, and she was thrilled to have us in her home (it had probably been a while since anyone else had been there!) but, because she had not experienced healthy nourishment and because she was out of touch with her own needs for nourishment, she had little to offer any of her guests.

· · · · · · · · · ·
Who's at the Top of Your List?

I once attended a pastor's conference in the beautiful mountains of Colorado, and one of the workshops was on personal priorities. The leader of the workshop, a pastor himself, encouraged each of us to put together a list of our basic priorities—our wives, our children, our jobs, our ministry, our hobbies. He then encouraged us to list those priorities in order of importance. When the lists were finished, we shared them with one another and talked about what we had each written.

Some of those attending the workshop felt it was important to put God at the top of the list. Others had their spouse or children at the top. After a time of discussion, the leader shared his own priority list, and it surprised most of us. In fact, at first glance the list seemed selfish. His first item was "spiritual health." His second item was "physical and emotional health." Needless to say, that prompted a lot of discussion during which the leader shared why he viewed his priorities in this way.

There was a time, he said, when he saw the people around him as being his first priority, and he had selflessly given his time and his energies to them. Time came, however, when he was completely worn out and disgusted with the people he was supposed to be serving. He also realized that his personal health was a shambles, and that was preventing him from having much to offer the people he was supposed to be serving. "I do consider those around me to be deserving of my commitment, but I have come to realize that if I don't have personal health and spiritual vitality, I don't have anything to give, and I'll fail in my assignment to serve."

It was a thoughtful lesson.

· · · · · · · · · ·
But Isn't All This Selfish?

So far I've emphasized the importance of personal nourishment because of the basic principle that if we are not nourished, we will not be able to live life to its fullest and will not be able to nourish others. I know some of you who are reading this book are going to respond to this discussion of personal nourishment by saying, "This all seems very selfish to me," just as Perry did. Some people are going to think that The Nourishment Factor caters to the pop-psychology emphasis on *me*.

Let me state categorically that I do not believe life should consist of being preoccupied with myself. As a Christian, I believe greater nourishment is going to be experienced by committing myself to others and to their needs. In order to do that, however, I need to be a nourished person. That's the plain and simple of it. The goal is to be a nourished person in the most basic way.

Additionally, I need to be committed to other people in a way that will either help them or allow them to be nourished as well. Many of us don't know how to respond to another person's need in a healthy way. A lot of us want to help others, but we are missing out because we make a lot of decisions that are not nourishing to either ourselves or those whom we want to help. The result is that some of us feel trapped or confined or obligated and, along with that, we feel a lot of resentment, especially if we have gotten burned out trying to help other people.

To illustrate what I mean, let me introduce you to three people—Mark Forbes, Sheila Woods, and William Chase.

· · · · · · · · · ·
Applying the Principle of Nourishment

Mark Forbes is a high-energy motivational speaker and financial advisor who has distinguished himself by his success in just about everything. He drives the right car, lives in the right condo, wears the right clothes, and hangs around with the beautiful people. Life with him is like being in a Hollywood movie.

William Chase is a pleasant, grandfather-type man who is well-educated, owns a successful business, and has become a fairly popular speaker for various organizations and churches. He is a severe critic of any discussion about "self." He does not believe people should pay attention to self-nourishment; he considers it to be anti-biblical.

Sheila Woods is the mother of three children and works as a clerk for a large corporation. She is known for her selfless life and can always be counted on to volunteer to work at the church. She smiles a lot but basically is a person living in chaos.

Let's look at each of these people from the perspective of nourishment, beginning with Mark Forbes, the high-energy motivational speaker.

In my view, Mark is the epitome of self-centeredness. He is not without the ability to be gracious when it serves his needs and he has been known to give lavish gifts. Either strings are attached to his gifts or the recipient feels the gift was intended to bring Mark some recognition. He is completely immersed in his own nourishment. In his case, it could be called selfishness.

I have known him for nearly twenty years and have never seen or heard of an occasion when he did something that was truly meant to nourish another person. Those who work with him merely tolerate him, and he'd probably have a lot fewer friends if he weren't so wealthy. He spends virtually every waking moment pursuing something that will serve his ego or his appetite for money.

The only nourishment Mark understands is visible, material nourishment. I'm not even sure how much emotional nourishment he experiences, and he certainly is not pursuing any spiritual nourishment.

Next is my opinionated friend William Chase. If he heard me having a discussion on the radio with someone like Sheila, he would be hopping mad about what he considers to be the emphasis on "self." He argues that the Christian choice is for others, not for ourselves.

The interesting thing about William is that he is one of the most intense people about making decisions on his own behalf that I know. He's really finicky about where he lives, what he wears, who does or does not intrude in his schedule, where he speaks, how much he is paid. He is, for example, a very good businessman because he knows when to make a decision in the best interests of his business. On more than one occasion when I have called him to ask him to be a guest on my program, he has not hesitated to either turn down my request or to delay responding to me because of some important priority in his personal life.

I remember one occasion, for example, when I asked him to guest host my radio program while I was on vacation. He turned down my request because he was going on vacation at the same time. Was that not a decision based on his own needs and interests? Yes! Was it a selfish decision? No! In fact, I wouldn't characterize him as a selfish man. He is very giving in many respects. He seems to be blinded, however, to the fact that what he probably considers to be wise and healthy decisions about his own life are ones that are based on a healthy understanding of personal nourishment. In my opinion it is hypocritical of him to criticize others who are struggling to achieve the same balance.

Sheila, my clerk friend who is in perpetual motion, is typical of many of us. She is an example of someone who wants to live a nourished life and also wants to nourish others, yet none of that seems to be happening. I cannot describe her life or the lives of her husband or children as well-nourished, even though she seems to be giving a lot of herself through her church and other volunteer activities. She is exhausted most of the time and complains bitterly about what needs to be done. Sheila needed to make the kinds of choices that would not only be nourishing to her and to her family, but which would also erect barriers to protect that nourishment.

· · · · · · · · · ·
New Choices and New Boundaries

"It is important for you to reach out and nourish others," I told Sheila as we discussed her chaotic schedule, "but you're going to have to do it in a way that truly helps and blesses them and in a way which won't turn you into a bitter volunteer."

"Right now I feel like moving to Siberia," she admitted.

"First, Sheila," I told her, "it is going to be important for you to realize that it is not your responsibility to respond to every need that comes your way. You need to admit to yourself, 'I can't do it all.' After coming to that realization, you need to ask yourself, 'Okay, if I can't do it all, what can I do? What choices should I make to help other people?' I think you would agree with me, Sheila, that your family should be the first to receive your help, and anything that would stand in the way of properly nourishing them is destructive. After making the right choices for you and your family, you need to think about how you can invest your life in the lives of others or in your community."

"But after I give to my family, there's no time left," she complained.

"It's possible, Sheila, that this season of your life is going to have to be focused on the needs of your family, and that is the investment in 'others' that is right for now. You may need to create an invisible boundary for yourself, which makes you and your family your top priority. You don't need to end your commitment to your church or to volunteer work. But those decisions are going to have to be made with your own nourishment and the nourishment of your family in mind. There is a point at which you need to establish the boundaries that will ensure the best for you, for your family, for those at the church, for your friends, for your relatives—for all those who are important to you.

"You can also reconsider another choice you've made," I continued.

"What is that?"

"How do you feel about your job?" I inquired.

"Well, it's a job. I don't love it, but the pay is good."

"Would you describe your career as nourishing?" I asked.

Sheila chuckled, "I wouldn't describe it as nourishing, and I wouldn't describe it as a career."

"Well, there's an opportunity for you to rethink your employment," I suggested.

"I'm not sure what you mean."

"Look at your circumstances, Sheila," I answered. "You are running yourself ragged trying to nourish other people by volunteering for activities that really don't fit your heart or your schedule, and you are spending forty hours a week working at a job you don't particularly like. In the middle of all that, neither you nor your family is being truly nourished."

"Yeah, that's right," she responded.

"I'd like to suggest that you find a job that allows you to help others. Why spend all day working at something you do not like, and then spend several evenings a week volunteering for activities you do like when you don't have time or energy for that and for your family too?"

"What kind of job are you suggesting?"

"There are hundreds of places that need people who want to give of themselves the way you do, places that deal with children and adults with special needs, places that pay attention to those in our society who fall through the cracks. I feel certain that you could find a position that would pay as much as you've been making (which wasn't very much) and would also satisfy your desire to help others."

Sheila was inspired by our conversation and later found a wonderful job working for a county in California as a victim's rights advocate. When someone suffered a violent crime, such as rape, or when a child was molested, Sheila became involved with the individual or family to assist them through the legal process, to help them receive the aid that was available to them, and to stand with them when they needed support.

Sheila was a person who needed to reevaluate the choices and boundaries in her life and to make new choices and set new boundaries that would benefit herself and others. To do so she needed to recognize the second principle of nourishment—"The responsibility for being nourished is mine"—which we will consider in Chapter 3.

CHAPTER 3

....

You Are Responsible for Your Own Nourishment

Mitch was a middle-aged businessman who had a reputation for being a kind, gentle-spirited person. It would be easy to think that he had the subject of nourishment all figured out because he was a very giving person.

One night I got a call from Mitch's wife. "He's falling apart, Rich. He thinks he's going crazy. He says he seriously wants to sell his company and move to Mexico."

As I hung up the phone I reflected on what I knew about him. He had a wonderful family. His business was doing well enough to pay the bills. I liked him a lot, and he was always easy to be with, but there was a part of Mitch that I did not know. I wondered if anyone knew.

Mitch and I got together over the next several weeks to talk about his desire to flee to Mexico. As I had suspected, there was more to Mitch than he ever let another person— or even himself—realize. Between the chats he and I had, and the time Mitch spent with the counselor I referred him to, he came to realize that he had been sexually molested by a favorite aunt during his childhood. Like many victims, he had blocked the events from his memory because they were just too painful to remember.

"I've never made a nourishing decision for myself in my life," Mitch admitted to me. "When I was a kid I felt like I had to make everyone happy, and that's what I did. I went to the college I thought everybody wanted me to attend. I married the girl I thought everybody wanted me to marry. I entered into the profession I thought everybody wanted me to pursue. I joined the church I thought everybody wanted me to join. I was a robot."

The feeling of helplessness had culminated in Mitch's desire to leave his business and move to Mexico. He had finally reached a point in life where making decisions on the basis of everybody else's expectation of him had collapsed on top of him. Even his reputation for being a giving person, he realized, had been based on his compulsive desire to give of himself even if that was in conflict with what would be right and healthy for his life, his family, and even for those whom he volunteered to help.

The first major principle of nourishment is that nourishment must begin with ourselves. The second principle places the responsibility for our own nourishment in our own court.

· · · · · · · · ·

The Responsibility for Being Nourished Is Mine

Each of us has the natural desire to live a nourished life. We sometimes have real problems, however, deciding who is responsible for our nourishment.

One reason is that each of us begins life totally dependent on another person for our nourishment. Babies need to be fed, typically by Mom, or they will not survive. As we grow older, we gradually assume more and more responsibility for our own nourishment. As children we learn to butter our own toast or to choose our own cereal. As teens we graduate to frying an egg or microwaving a hot dog. Eventually we reach the stage of total personal responsibility—the essential burden for whether we are healthy and eating well rests on our own shoulders.

That's easy to understand when it comes to physical nourishment, but many of us have trouble with this principle as it relates to other kinds of nourishment. Especially victims of physical, mental, or verbal abuse, like Mitch, who have been thrust into adult life with the knowledge that those who were supposed to provide for them did not do so have difficulty recognizing their personal responsibility. They unconsciously think, *I deserve to be fed. I should have been fed. I don't feel I've ever been fed so you'd better feed me.*

There is nothing whatever wrong with having the hunger to be nourished by those around us. That desire is from God. Even though adults have reached the point in their lives where they are carrying the responsibility for their own nourishment, they still have the privilege of being nourished by other people. Husbands and wives nourish one another. Friends nourish one another. Parents and children nourish one another.

It is important to recognize, however, that even though we are to be nourished by others, and even though we don't need to apologize for our desire for that to happen, *the basic responsibility for whether or not we are nourished persons is ours—not anyone else's.*

Gloria and Mike attended the same church as we did. She was the daughter of some old friends from my college days. They had been married for about two years, just long enough to begin to realize that the honeymoon does not last forever. From outside appearances the marriage seemed to be made in heaven. That was only the view from the outside, however.

One day Gloria asked if we could get together to talk about some of what was happening in their home.

"I admired Mike for a long time before he got interested in me and we married," Gloria told me. "He was the good-looking, star athlete who seemed to be 'Mr. Wonderful.' I was the small-town girl who was anxious for someone to sweep me off my feet," Gloria said as she explained how they met and revealed something of their courtship days. "Mike's still a really wonderful person, and there is a lot about him that I love, but he's just not very sensitive."

"What do you mean, Gloria?" I asked.

"Well, in little things mostly," she replied. "He's a good provider and committed to the Lord, but I feel that he just doesn't care about some of my needs."

"For example?" I prompted.

"Let me tell you about our anniversary," she answered. "He told me that he had a surprise planned. I got excited and wondered what he might have in mind. I was looking forward to doing something like going out for dinner or spending the weekend alone, just the two of us.

"When the big day came, he gave me an anniversary card with two tickets to a baseball game. That's where we spent the evening of our anniversary—sitting on the bleachers at a baseball stadium, eating hot dogs, and dodging drunks."

"How did you react to that?"

"I was so angry I could have smeared him with the mustard from my hot dog," Gloria replied. "I was embarrassed for him too. If people around us had known that it was our anniversary, and that he had chosen to take me to a baseball game to celebrate, he would have been hissed and booed out of the stadium."

Many of us respond to other people's disregard for our natural hunger for love with anger, just as Gloria did. Often our actions are motivated by our underlying hungers.

Kinds of Hunger

The list of various hungers in our lives could be endless but I think it is helpful to group them under two broad categories: the hunger for love and the hunger for approval. I have written about this in greater detail in my book *Love, No Strings Attached,* but let me summarize it for the purpose of our discussion about nourishment.

Love

There is an instinct in each of us that cries out for unconditional acceptance. There is a hunger that says, "Please love me the way I am and don't take my faults and failures into account. Please ignore whether my teeth are straight or crooked or whether I get good grades in school or whether I'm fat or skinny or whether I'm neat or sloppy. Please give me the assurance that you can momentarily set aside my failures or even set aside my successes or my possessions or my beauty and love me just because I'm me. That way I will know that if any of those factors change, you will still love me."

I define love as "anything that is done for another person because of who that person is." Love has nothing to do with what that person has done or not done. It is offered because that person exists and is an object of my love. The hunger for that kind of love is powerful and natural. It is as instinctive as the craving for water or food and can only be truly satisfied by unconditional love.

Approval

Love is unconditional and cannot be earned and, therefore, cannot be lost. Approval, however, is completely conditional and can be lost because it is based on performance. I need approval from those who are the most important to me in order to know "how I'm doing" in my culture. Am I performing correctly? Am I doing okay? Am I attractive? Is there something that I need to improve in order to receive approval?

The desire to be approved is natural to people throughout the world, but the nature of how we attain approval will be different from person to person, home to home, group to group, and culture to culture.

Just as all of us do, Gloria longed for love, and she told me other stories about how Mike had disappointed her on special occasions.

"There is nothing wrong with what you want," I told Gloria, acknowledging her natural desire for love. "Mike is supposed to be a source of nourishment for you. Perhaps he does need to think about sensitivity. But let me ask you an important question."

"Okay," she said.

"Before your anniversary, did you talk with Mike about what you wanted?'"

"No," Gloria answered quietly.

"Why not?"

"I don't know," Gloria admitted. Then she shrugged her shoulders and said, "I guess I wanted him to come up with the idea himself. I didn't want him to do something simply because I asked. It wouldn't seem very natural."

"There is an important principle involved in living a nourished life," I told Gloria. "The basic responsibility for being nourished is yours, not anybody else's. If you wanted to celebrate your anniversary with an intimate dinner for two, the responsibility for expressing that wish, and perhaps even doing something to make it happen, was yours. You really did yourself, and Mike, a disservice by being reluctant to talk about that with him."

"But what if he didn't want to do what I wished?" she asked.

"Then you and he would need to talk; you might even

have to reach a compromise. But at least you would have been helping Mike to do something nourishing for you. That's what I mean by bearing the responsibility for your own nourishment."

Sometimes, however, we don't feel eligible to be nourished. Then we see ourselves as victims, as Mitch, the man who wanted to escape to Mexico, saw himself.

· · · · · · · · ·

Sometimes We Don't Feel Eligible

"It's an eligibility issue," I told Mitch. "Victims do not feel eligible for good things. For you to have said 'no' to someone who wanted your help would have seemed selfish to you. For you to have said 'yes' to something that would have been better for you would have seemed selfish. You even have a hard time making right decisions about the growth of your business because a part of you does not feel eligible to succeed."

It is easy for many of us, especially those who have experienced victimization, to have the feeling, "Life is nourishing for everybody except me." Other people seem to have the things we hunger for so deeply. Compared to them we feel unlucky, and we resent the fact that God or life or fate has been good to them and not to us. We keep living for the day when it will be our turn to have what they have. We feel a form of powerlessness and helplessness and the sense that nothing will ever change. We think:

- My marriage is a trap.
- My job is a dead end.
- My life is irreparably doomed.

Many victims feel personally responsible for their victimization. They carry a responsibility that is not theirs, and they fail to place the responsibility on the shoulders of the perpetrator where it belongs. This contributes to their helplessness. Without putting this feeling into words they think, *I am bad. Bad things have always happened to me. Why should I try to improve anything? It will all end up bad again.*

The Lies Victims Believe

Multitudes of emotionally and spiritually emaciated people end up sitting in a window, watching all the people walk by who are nourished in ways for which they are hungry. They really believe that the only difference between themselves and the other people is that the others have been honored with health and good looks and intelligence.

Imagine a person who lives in a prosperous culture where everyone around him is well fed, but he is in the throes of starvation, his hair falling out, his bones protruding from his skin. He sits in the window watching people go by who are robust and hardy.

Imagine the trap the starving man is in if, as he sits in his window, he thinks to himself that his intense hunger and the pain and discomfort of his condition are simply his lot in life; the only option available to him is to try very hard to discover the magic or the curse that explains the difference. For him nourishment is not found by walking a practical pathway; it is something he believes just happens to the right people. It's a prize for being lucky. Looking fit and nourished is a trophy that says, "I'm one of the beautiful people and some of us have got it and some of us don't."

So there he sits day after day waiting for the time he will finally look in the mirror and see something in himself that looks like the others. While he waits, nourishment is just outside his door or around the corner or down the street or maybe even in the next room. The only reason the other people look and act the way they do is because they have made nourishing choices day after day. They have had breakfast, lunch, dinner, and snacks. They have chosen a variety of nutritious foods to eat.

There is a pathway, steps he can take that will lead him

toward what he wants, but he doesn't take any of them because he doesn't realize that nourishment comes from the choices he makes. Yes, he feels a form of responsibility for his condition, but it is the weight of "being" the wrong kind of person rather than having failed to "do" the right things that he hasn't begun to understand.

In his thinking, the pathway is only filled with nourished people and since he is not nourished he is not ready to step onto the pathway. No amount of urging will make him venture out from his window, because every time he tries, he has the feeling, "I'm not one of them, and until I feel and look like one of them I'm not going to go out among them."

I have a friend whom I have watched go through this for years. Jack is almost forty years old, is married, and has one child. He works in a warehouse of a large grocery chain and makes good pay, but he hates the job. Since childhood Jack has wanted to be a forest ranger. It's been his dream and his passion. He has collected books and magazine articles and brochures about the subject and be-friended every forest ranger he can find.

I first met Jack after the Sunday morning service at a church I pastored. He came up to me as I was standing in the parking lot finishing a conversation with a member of the church.

"I'm going to start attending your church," he an-nounced. "I'm looking for a new church home and I really enjoyed this morning's service."

"I'm happy to hear that," I replied. "Tell me about your-self."

Jack briefed me about his life and his family, then said, "I'm working for a market chain right now, but I'm hoping to get a job as a forest ranger in northern California."

I commented on what an interesting field that would be, and we chatted about it a little before we both had to leave for Sunday lunch.

About every six months or so after that, Jack would either catch me after a church service or make an appointment to come into the office and talk about how much he longed to become a forest ranger and how things in his life didn't seem to be going in that direction. He felt stuck and resentful.

The more Jack and I talked about his dream of being a forest ranger, the more I came to realize that he was not taking any meaningful steps toward that goal.

As I reflected on my conversations with Jack, I realized he didn't understand that forest rangers were people very much like himself who have walked particular pathways in order to get where they are. He was like that starving man in the window who longingly watches all the people walk by who are the way he wants to be, but if he steps outside the door to join them, he is so overwhelmed by how much he is not like them that he jumps back inside and resents what seems to be the "divine plan" that blocks him from his goal.

The root of this feeling is, most often, some form of childhood destruction. During one particularly significant conversation, Jack revealed his experience.

"Jack," I probed, "in my experience the kind of disqualification and ineligibility you are experiencing is associated with deep destruction, especially in the early years of your life. Does that ring any bells for you?"

"Like what?"

Because of some other things Jack had said to me during previous conversations, I suspected sexual abuse so that was where I started. "Was there ever a time in your childhood when there was any kind of sexual contact between you and an adult?"

Jack started perspiring profusely and had a very difficult time responding to my question. Finally he told me about repeated occasions of incest with his mother, something he had never admitted to anyone before and, until that day, did not know was considered molestation, even though he had always felt uncomfortable about it.

In reality a person like Jack needs to come to the point where he can see the truth of what happened: Somebody else did something to me that should never have been done. Then there can be a response to what happened that is more real—anger and tears and hurt and all the confusing emotions that come with being betrayed. Yet the tears don't need to last forever. Once he realizes that it was not his fault after all, he can stop carrying the burden. He can hold the person who hurt him accountable.

The result is I can now understand I am responsible for what happens from now on, not the perpetrator and what that person did. That can be good news!

· · · · · · · · · ·

I'm Responsible for My Own Life

We begin brand new lives when we realize the responsibility for what happens to us is ours—no one else's. Now we realize:

- I don't need to be hopelessly handcuffed to whatever failures occurred in my childhood home.
- I don't need to blame the people who have hurt me and let me down, or my teachers, or the government.
- I don't have to hold my spouse or my friends responsible if I am essentially living a malnourished life.
- Yes, my relatives or my friends have failed me. Yes, a lot of disgusting things have happened to me. Yes, I've experienced treachery and betrayal. Yes, some of those people should be held accountable for it. But the decision of what will happen to me now, and whether my next choices are going to be nourishing to me, is mine and mine alone. If I get to the end of a day or a month or a year without nourishment, it is my fault and mine alone.

When I say we must bear responsibility for our own nourishment, that does not have to be interpreted as a heavy task someone has placed on our backs. To the contrary, it's good news. The load of believing nothing can change, that we are still small, powerless children who cannot make choices of healing and fulfillment, has been removed.

Picture it this way: What was once an enormous and crippling heap strapped to your back has been exchanged for something else that is still on your shoulders—a well-fitted, comfortable vest that contains the tools for living.

I once heard a wise man say, "If your friends have hurt you, that's their fault. Being held back by it—that's your fault."

This does not mean that we ignore the betrayals and the hurts or try to diminish or hide them. Some of us have stuffed our pain into a compartment somewhere and developed a way of living that says, "I'm not going to think about this, talk about it, or solve it." We mistakenly think that ignoring our pain is the best way of handling it. We may even say to ourselves and others, "I'm not going to dwell on the past. I want to get on with the future."

Those nice words often mean the debris from that pain is going to continue to affect our lives and the lives of those around us. No, we don't want to dwell on the past or be preoccupied with it anymore than we want to live the rest of our lives in a hospital bed or a body cast. But a "season" of treating our wounds is the way to see them healed. I talked about that season in my book *Pain and Pretending;* reading this book is one way that may help you walk through this time successfully. Many people, like Mitch and Jack, may also need counseling to understand how the pain in their past is effecting their everyday decisions.

Mitch had to go through a very difficult but life-changing season of dealing with the roots of his victimization and grieving about all the decisions he had made for his life that had not been from his heart. That didn't mean, however, that he divorced his wife, just because he realized the inadequacy of his original commitment to her. He came to the point where he could make a fresh and more healthy commitment to her. He started experimenting with personally nourishing decisions and was not only healthier, but his business improved as well. Now, he enjoys helping others a lot more because when his heart says "yes," he really means it.

I don't know if Jack will ever achieve his goal of becoming a forest ranger. Frankly, I hope he will. I do know this will only happen if he recognizes that there is no mystery to living a nourished life. Like those around him, he can explore pathways and choose to walk the paths that lead to his nourishment.

· · · · · · · · ·

An Added Word of Caution

One other warning about sitting along the sidelines of other people's pathways and watching them with helpless envy: a malnourished person will not only become preoccupied with hunger and pain, but also with the people who have what he doesn't have. There will be the inner thought, *I don't have what he has, but if I can become like him, I will succeed.* We can become obsessed with trying to duplicate another person's life or constantly measure ourselves using that person, or people like him or her, as the only yardstick to measure fulfillment. Many people's lives have been spent trying to measure up to big sister or Mom or Dad or a successful or beautiful friend.

As you watch other people along the pathway of life, and as you become conscious of your own hunger and malnourishment, it will be counterproductive to try to become someone else. That can produce a life of stuffing cushions in your clothes so your thin frame can look fit, or wearing wigs to hide the loss of your hair, or plastering layers of makeup on your face trying to look healthy and rosy. Even if you do start taking steps toward nourishment, you might be dissatisfied with what you've got because you still don't look like the person or persons you have defined as your model.

It's good to be inspired by others, but the result of the inspiration should be for us to dream and to pursue our own dreams. The goal is to be nourished, to have finally the confidence and the satisfaction of being one of the people on the pathway who has muscle and tone and brightness. But we must remember: it's my muscle, my tone, my own unique brightness, not anyone else's. All the people on the pathway have two things in common—hunger and the opportunity for nourishment. Everything else is distinctive and special. All anyone needs is to be a *nourished me*, not a manufactured *replica of you*.

What is your dream? Is it to have a better marriage or a good job or to enjoy friendship with others? Don't sit along the sidelines of other people's pathways, enviously thinking that something fundamental disqualifies you from nourishment. Explore and step out. Read a book or attend a seminar. But be careful. Sometimes you can read hundreds of books and still be stuck on the pathway. Books, seminars, tapes and other sources of information are merely ways to explore the actual steps to take. A step usually involves some disclosure of yourself to a spouse or a friend or a counselor or a group. It also involves setting some new boundaries, such as establishing a rule that ever so often you and your spouse will get away for a nourishing weekend or a dinner out with one of your children or that you will make time to pursue an interest or hobby.

. . . .
God and Miracles

"But where is God in all this? Doesn't he answer prayer? Does everything depend on me? Doesn't God perform miracles?"

God is walking the pathway with us, and his involvement in our choices and experiences along the way is extensive. He delights in demonstrating his love for us and his power to help us. Each of us can experience wonderful miracles in our relationship with him and times of supernatural direction.

We need to remind ourselves, however, that he is the one who has placed us in a world where pathways lead to what we want and need. He has promised that, if we acknowledge him in every way, he will direct our paths. Sometimes he supernaturally shows us a particular pathway to take, and other times he lets us choose based on what he has communicated to us or helped us learn through experience. There will be miracles because that's a part of knowing and following God, but miracles will not be a substitute for being a pathfinder.

Whenever we feel stuck and look around us at people who seem to have what we want, and we are tempted to feel that they just *got it* from somewhere and we *didn't get it*, we need to remind ourselves of a basic truth of nourishment. We will arrive at what we want and need by discovering the course that will lead to satisfaction and fulfillment.

Why not discover the pathways? Why not take steps toward your dream!

CHAPTER 4

. . . .

Your Nourishment Should Come from More Than One Source

I once worked with a fellow named Willie who had a knack for finding and experimenting with every wacky diet that came along. Something within him rebelled against generally accepted ways of eating. Balanced nutrition was as foreign to him as Swahili.

I have memories of Willie walking into the office with a continually changing supply of bags, pails, plastic bowls, and boxes, which contained assorted gadgets to mix, blend, fold, and liquefy his culinary experiments. He offered long explanations about his food choices, saying that they would do everything from clean his liver to rejuvenate his brain cells.

Actually, I don't have any trouble with the notion that certain unusual substances might have beneficial effects on the body, but Willie went to extremes; he would eat just one particular kind of food or drink only one kind of juice for extended periods of time. One time he ate only avocados. He had them for breakfast, lunch, dinner, and snacks.

He mashed them, sliced them, pureed them, and fried them. Someone had convinced him that eating nothing but avocados for a month would cleanse him of impurities. I jokingly began to call him "Guacamole."

The most memorable of Willie's excursions into the nether world of food came the day he read in a magazine that carrots would rejuvenate his aging brain. Whether that is true or not, I don't know, but I doubt that the article meant for a person to eat only carrots. Willie, however, had the attitude that if a little bit helped, a lot would do wonders, so he embarked upon a season of his life during which he ate nothing but carrots. He had sliced carrots to munch on while he was at work. He created slaws and salads from carrots. He fried them in butter, smothered them in soy sauce, and even boiled and mashed them.

Whenever Willie embarked on one of these projects he would usually get quite excited about the results he seemed to be getting. During the carrot venture he swore his brain was working better and his memory was improved (which he demonstrated by memorizing a lengthy poem). Willie decided to continue with the carrot diet as long as possible.

After several weeks, Willie's breath started smelling bad, and unusual body odors developed. Even though he may have gone through a period when he felt his brain was working better, his other processes began to deteriorate. Willie started appearing sluggish in his movements, and his mental sharpness was definitely getting dull. The frustrating part was that Willie didn't realize any of this and still convinced himself that he was doing wonderfully well. No matter how much we all tried to encourage Willie to start eating normally again, he resisted. It began to look as though this experiment was going to end in disaster.

The end finally came in an unexpected way. Some of us started noticing that Willie was beginning to look like a carrot! No, it wasn't delusion on our part. His skin had actually taken on an orange tinge. At first, he didn't believe us and couldn't see it in the mirror, but enough people began expressing concern over his appearance that he got scared and went to a doctor. There he learned that a substance in carrots called, appropriately enough, carotene, can actually affect skin color if you eat enough carrots over a long enough period of time. The doctor was finally able to convince Willie to start eating normally again, at least for a while.

As you might guess, Willie had more peculiarities than just his diet. He was the kind of person who was psychologically vulnerable to way-out notions; I admit that not many people would do the same thing. Most of us know enough about nutrition to choose a variety of things to eat, and even if we are ignorant about nutrition, we have a natural desire to experience variety in taste and color. Few of us would eat just one or two foods for any length of time unless we were forced to because there was nothing else available.

When it comes to invisible nourishment, however, vast numbers of us are living like Willie, relying on one or two sources of sustenance. Another important principle of nourishment is: Nourishment does not come from one source.

· · · · · · · · ·

Nourishment Does Not Come from One Source

Think about it. We each have a limitless number of sources of nourishment. We should receive nourishment from our friends and family, our jobs and schools, our fellowship with other Christians and God's word, our hobbies, our enjoyment of nature, and the various colors and tastes and sensations in the world around us. Sometimes, however, especially in times of deep pain and when we feel failure or fear, our individual worlds can get smaller and smaller and our sources of nourishment become fewer and fewer in number until we reach the point of having, literally, only one or two sources left.

We then begin to expect our hungers to be satisfied by only one or two sources of nourishment. This diminished state is one of the causes of addiction. An addict can sometimes be described as a desperately hungry person who does not have a broad number of rich sources for nourishment and, therefore, clings to whatever limited sources of nourishment are left.

Doreen, a woman I met at a retreat in the mountains, is an example of what I'm describing. Doreen wanted to talk with me about a weight problem.

"I have tried to lose weight over and over again," she told me. "I am sometimes successful, but it always seems to come back, and I feel like I'm really failing the Lord by not being able to control it."

As we talked it became clear that, even though Doreen's weight problem was going to be an obstacle for some men to overcome, it was not her only obstacle to finding and keeping a boyfriend. From the intensity of her conversation with me, it was not hard for me to imagine her as a person who could smother someone close to her.

"Doreen, you don't have just a weight problem," I told her after she had had the opportunity to tell most of her story. "You have an eating disorder. Getting help from a counselor or a program that deals with eating disorders will be a helpful next step. It is easy for you to feel that your eating is 'the problem,' but it is not. It is a symptom of other issues. I think you'll also discover some insights that will help with relationships with friends and boyfriends as well."

I did a little probing and discovered, not to my surprise, that Doreen had been reared in an abusive home. Her mother was a rageaholic who was angry most of the time and had abused her both physically and emotionally. Her father was the type of person who just didn't seem to know what to do about the situation. As a result, emotionally Doreen lived in a very tiny world.

Picture Doreen as a teenager. Instead of getting up in the morning in a house where she was loved and accepted, instead of looking forward to seeing friends and going to a school where some academic or other activities were nourishing to her, instead of receiving nourishment from teachers or administrators in school, she got up in the morning with very little to anticipate.

It wasn't that she didn't have friends or activities. She was a very social person during her school years and participated in various extracurricular projects, such as acting and singing in the high school chorus. She was driven to try to be perfect, however, so none of those activities was very nourishing to her.

At a time when very little made sense to her, at a time when she was starved for nourishment, Doreen discovered one wonderful source of satisfaction: food—bread and milk and chocolate and hamburgers and milk shakes and a host of other yummy treats. She soon developed the reputation of a big eater. Yet the goodies she ate in public were nothing compared to what she gobbled in secret. She would go on binges during which she would eat massive quantities of cakes or candy. She remembered being home alone and making enough peanut butter and jelly sandwiches to make an entire loaf of bread disappear. Doreen had only one source of nourishment—food, and her craving for nourishment led her overeating to become an addiction.

Doreen was starved for natural and good things, but in her starvation, she discovered only one source of daily feeding, and that was food. The tragedy was that those huge quantities of food would not feed her emotionally and spiritually. Additionally, that which was supposed to be a delightful, normal source of nourishment for her life—the partaking of food—became a tormented and guilt-ridden activity, which was hard to bring into balance.

"You see, Doreen, you don't have to resent your hunger, and you don't have to hate food. Your childhood experiences have led you to use food to satisfy all of the hungers of your life, but God did not design food to play that role. Food is meant to be just one of many rich sources of nourishment."

Doreen is an example of those of us who have, because of pain and fear and guilt, ended up living in a tiny world. In a world like Doreen's almost anything that is available becomes one of the few sources of nourishment and pleasure. We gasp for it. It becomes an addiction, a sad substitute for living a broadly nourished life. Many addictions are physiological—overeating, excessive drinking, drug use, or promiscuity, even addictions to seemingly good things such as exercise or other forms of physical pleasure. For some of us our bodies are all that is left in our world. Almost everything outside of our bodies seems to be cut off from us or represents risk or failure. Under those circumstances it is easy to resent our hunger and to think of food or sex as always evil.

Part of our recovery process is the joyful discovery that we don't need to resent our hungers. Food and drink and sex and hobbies and achievement all fit into the balance of our lives.

· · · · · · · · ·

Balance

We often say it is important to have a balanced diet when we talk about our physical bodies. Meats, vegetables, fruits, dairy products, nuts, beverages all contribute to a well-balanced, nutritious diet. Even within the different categories of foods, there is variety. For example, beef and pork and lamb and poultry are different kinds of meat.

Most of us know we should eat different foods, and listen to our bodies carefully so we will sense what kind of foods we are craving. We look for balance as we nourish our bodies.

That word, *balance*, is also important to our emotional and spiritual lives. Balance in a person's life is best evaluated by looking at activities that have spanned a period of time such as weeks or months.

I once received a telephone call on my program from a woman who was upset with her husband because he had made the decision to go fishing over the weekend with a group of his buddies.

"He claims that his wife and his children are his top priority," she said, "but then he abandons us to do something with other people."

"The real question," I told her, "is not whether it was right for your husband to go fishing for the weekend. That one trip does not mean that he doesn't love his family. We need to look at his choices over a period of several months. If this trip is just one of many, and if it is obvious that fishing and other activities are his top priority, then we could say there was a real problem."

Balance can still be achieved, even when situations within a short time period seem to be imbalanced. To use the food example once again, you don't need to feel guilty about having eaten fish two or three days in a row, even though you know that your overall diet should not consist entirely of fish. You'll balance things out with future meals. In the same way, none of us should feel guilty for committing time to a job or to a hobby or to helping a friend or to a vacation if we are engaged in other activities over a longer period of time.

I recently returned from vacation, for example. My family and I spend at least a week every year camping, fishing, hiking, enjoying the wilderness, and reading and talking with friends who vacation with us. No office, no telephones, no deadlines, no "work" in the professional sense. How out of balance can you get! Yet it is a part of achieving overall balance for our lives. If I spent the entire year camping, that would be out of balance. If I consistently ignored my responsibilities to my family and my job in order to camp and fish, that would not be healthy. But it is healthy occasionally to equalize some of the things in my life by experiencing other forms of nourishment and recreation.

Think about your own life. Even if you are a social person or an achieving person, what do you *really* rely on for nourishment? What are you living for each day? Are there multiple sources of nourishment in your life, or are you expecting just one or two people or activities or even substances to carry you along?

· · · · · · · · ·

Other Options for Nourishment

If you have chosen only one or two sources of nourishment, you need to consider new options to help to satisfy your hunger.

New Relationships

It's easy for us to think of someone who is nourished by one or two sources as a person who lives a very strange and secluded life, who lurks in a dark apartment somewhere watching television and doing little else. Some people are like that. But I've found that many people are like Mary Ann who, from all appearances, was a successful, outgoing person.

Mary Ann had experienced the trauma of divorce when she was forty. Still that hadn't stopped her. She had returned to college, graduated, and ultimately became a management consultant. She was quite good at what she did and developed an excellent reputation in her field. I first became acquainted with her when she sent me a copy of a book she had written about home management, and I invited her to be a guest on my radio program.

Late one afternoon as I was about to leave the radio station, I received a call from Mary Ann. She asked if I would give her some advice about her private life.

Mary Ann took a long time to tell me about the unhappiness of her childhood and her adolescent years. Her home had been an unhappy place for a child, and her relationship with her father had not been good. The failed marriage had been only one of numerous intense relationships with men, all of which had collapsed.

"Mary Ann, what sources of emotional and spiritual nourishment do you have in your life?" I asked.

She spent some time discussing that with me, and finally realized that, even though she had the reputation of being a social, successful person, much of her activity was not really nourishing to her.

"I guess I get some kind of nourishment from my career," she said, "but another part of me has been tormented. I like it when I succeed, but in the loneliness of my own bedroom it doesn't seem to have real meaning to me."

As we talked, it became clear that Mary Ann was a desperately hungry person who had tried to satisfy her hunger with achievement in career or school and relationships with men, two very limited sources.

"I've smothered the guys I've been with," she reflected. "I've known it, and they have sometimes told me I overwhelm them with my needs, but I can't seem to stop. I am so hungry for closeness, I can't live without it. Then, when I become close to someone, I destroy the relationship."

"One of the obvious steps," I counseled, "is to uncover your hurts and wounds through counseling so you can experience healing at those deep levels. I also recommend, however, that you begin to realize how much you need nourishment from various sources and begin to take steps to find it."

"For example?" she questioned.

"Do you have any close female friends?" I asked.

Mary Ann went through a list of women she knew or had professional relationships with, but she admitted not one was an intimate chum.

"I can't tell you how often I find that a person who is having trouble with relationships with the opposite sex also does not have healthy friendships with the same sex," I told her. "Having an intimate association with friends of the same sex is one of the most important sources of nourishment in our lives. The healthy ways you interact with these friends can also be used in your relationships with the opposite sex."

"I've been so focused on my career and on men, I haven't had time for any other close or demanding relationships. I'm not even sure I want that," Mary Ann protested.

"I understand your concern, and I'm not suggesting that you manufacture close friendships. Just be aware of how you've limited your sources of nourishment.

"There's another area of nourishment that you should also consider, an area I consider to be foundational to a healthy life: spiritual nourishment."

Spiritual Nourishment

The normal Christian life is to be one with diverse sources of nourishment. Some of them are deep and lasting. Others are brief and temporary. Yet God intends for our lives to be sustained and blessed by the rich assortment he has provided.

Mary Ann told me she was part of a very respected church in her city and had even been a leader in that church. The more we talked about that, however, the more she realized she had been a part of the church because of a vague conviction that she "should" belong to a church, not because this church was spiritually nourishing to her. She admitted that she had attended other churches and had considered attending one she had visited with a friend a few weeks ago. "I really felt God's presence there," she told me.

"That's an important new choice for you to make," I told Mary Ann, "the sooner, the better."

Mary Ann is typical of a number of Christians who attend church weekly but receive no spiritual nourishment from the experience. We'll talk about why this occurs in Part Four, when we talk specifically about spiritual nourishment.

I am not concerned only about the individual who has come to live a life of limited personal nourishment, however. I am also concerned about subcultures, some of which are Christian, who view the world as having only limited opportunities for nourishment.

Some Christians Reject Other Nourishment

Some Christians have cut themselves off from realms of music and art and recreation and fun and science and entertainment and vocational pursuits, because they don't seem to be "Christian." Their children have been reared in religious environments that pretend as though seventy-five percent of the world around them doesn't exist.

I'm not saying that every choice is a good one. I am saying, however, that the size of the world in which we can learn and grow and enjoy ourselves is much larger than some of us realize. Many Christians have concluded that spiritual nourishment is the only nourishment a person needs. Their world has become one of church and study and Christian books and magazines—exclusively. This narrow focus has not only diminished their own nourishment, it has also hindered their ability to be nourishing to the larger world.

It's a frustrating position to be in, because, on the one hand we are being told that spiritual activities are all that we need for life, while on the other hand, our instincts are saying, "I'm not really feeling totally nourished by this, but I'm afraid to say so."

Just as Willie did, we are ignoring the obvious. All our nourishment cannot come from one source.

CHAPTER 5

· · · · · · · · · · · · ·

Everything That
Tastes Good Is
Not Always Nourishing

I worked for several years in the news media in Los Angeles. I remember vividly one of the more unusual stories I covered, which involved a very large, East Los Angeles family who had an enormous party for friends and neighbors and relatives one weekend. The event was stupendous. The whole street was blocked off, and more than three hundred people enjoyed food, dancing, and music. Unfortunately, the family had not gotten police permission to block off the street, and not every neighbor had been invited or even informed of the event, so a lot of tempers flared as residents tried to get into or out of their homes or tried to shield themselves from the noise. The party turned into a brawl, a great news story for an otherwise dull weekend.

The big story came the next day when dozens of those who attended the party started getting ill, some of them severely enough to be hospitalized. The authorities quickly realized that the illnesses were probably caused by something in the food at the party, and the problem finally was traced to a sauce that had not been properly prepared. Nobody died from the food poisoning, but a couple of people almost did. It was a party those folks would long remember; some of them undoubtedly came away from the experience with an increased interest in well-cooked food.

Now think about that feast. Some of the foods on the table were probably very nutritious. Some not so nutritious. Some of the food, even poisonous. At the time of the party, however, not too many people were thinking about whether or not the food would sustain life or promote growth. They certainly were not thinking that anything in front of them would be poisonous. The nourishment that day was good fun, good relations, and good-tasting food. It was tragically and unexpectedly interrupted by the poison.

Poison is as easily disguised in relationships with other people as it is in food. One woman I met recently when I taught a series of Sunday morning classes at a large church in southern California found this out.

The Woman Who Refused to See the Truth

At the close of the final session of my classes Marsha approached me and asked if I would talk with her for a while.

"I'm praying for my husband, Mark, to become a Christian," she began. "I'm asking the Lord to give me his strength to be the kind of wife my husband needs."

So far it sounded as if Marsha were a precious Christian wife who was really concerned for her non-Christian husband. "How can I help you?" I wondered out loud.

"Mark doesn't have any interest in my faith. He doesn't even like me to attend church. He sometimes listens to you on the radio so he let me attend your series, but I'm supposed to stop attending church after today."

As Marsha continued to talk about her relationship with

her husband I realized that he was treating her disrespect-fully and perhaps, abusively. It is common for a spouse in this type of relationship to be blinded to what is really oc-curring so I decided to ask a blunt yet very pertinent ques-tion.

"Marsha, has Mark ever hit you?"

The expression on Marsha's face instantly changed from a pleasant, concerned look to one of panic and confusion. "Why do you ask that?"

"Because you are describing very disrespectful behav-ior, and I'm wondering how far that disrespect has gone."

Marsha looked at the floor for a while, then without looking up she said, "He doesn't hit me very much, just when he gets angry."

"How often is that?" I pressed further.

"Maybe every couple of months," she admitted. "But he's really a nice person at times," she hastened to add.

"Have you ever told anyone about the way your hus-band treats you?"

"No," Marsha said quietly. "I have hoped that things would get better if I learned to be the kind of wife who could help him with his problems."

"Marsha, your situation sounds like domestic violence to me. I know that you love Mark, and you want your mar-riage to be successful. But that will not happen until his abusive behavior is recognized for what it is. You need to get help from a counselor who specializes in abuse."

Before their marriage Marsha had thought that Mark was a matrimonial feast. He was good looking, had a good job, and gave her the kind of attention she craved. It all seemed so nourishing! There were some warning signs along the way—signals from her parents and friends that she was walking into trouble—but she would not allow her-self to recognize them. All she knew was that their relation-ship seemed good and she wanted it. I would side with her parents and friends: the relationship was poisonous.

The simple question is, then, "How do I know whether something that is appealing, that I think will satisfy my appetite, is constructive or destructive?" This is especially important when it comes to emotional and spiritual nourishment because if we are deeply hungry and searching for something to satisfy our hunger, it is easy to think that the next thing that "tastes good" is the answer.

The goal of The Nourishment Factor is to learn to make healthy choices for our own lives and the lives of others. Much of the time, that is not a difficult challenge. If I am hungry, there is a whole range of foods that would appeal to me and which would satisfy my hunger. The problem is that there is also a whole range of foods which would not be nourishing, although they may satisfy my immediate hunger. Some of them, in fact, could even be destructive or poisonous. That means that not everything that tastes good is necessarily nourishing; I can't use simple taste or the immediate satisfaction of my hunger as evidence that I am being nourished.

Our Own Experience

Some of the ways that we learn what is or is not nourishing are obvious. As children we trust our parents or others around us to make nourishing choices on our behalf. Then we gradually learn from our own experience.

I suspect that Marsha had been overpowered as a child, perhaps by one or both of her parents, or she would have called a halt to Mike's behavior much sooner. Physical abuse probably seemed normal to her, whereas it wouldn't to a woman whose childhood experience had been healthy.

Our previous experience can help us determine whether or not something is nourishing. We will also discover that there are people around us, either friends or nutritional professionals, whom we can trust for good information.

Advice of Others

If we're smart, we don't have to pick some poisonous mushrooms and eat them in order to learn about them. Other people have already collected that kind of information and can be of immense help to us—if we'll trust them.

It all adds up to accumulating good information and always being alert for anything new that we need to know. In other words: *we learn to make good choices.* We are taught or we discover how as we grow and assume responsibility for our own nourishment. The ability to make good choices is not something that is mystically passed along to us genetically. It is not a matter of luck. It isn't even a matter of whether God loves us. If you want to live a nourished life, you must make nourishing choices. It's a practical reality. If you do not make nourishing choices, you'll either feel hunger or pain. That's a practical reality too.

"But I'd Rather Do It Myself"

Unfortunately many of us have the attitude expressed in a well-known T.V. commercial several years ago, ". . . Mother, please. I'd rather do it myself."

Yet getting good advice could be considered a kind of nourishment in itself. When we're faced with a career change or trying to decide what kind of car to buy or how to handle conflict in marriage, someone who has already gone through those choices (even if the choices proved to be wrong), can give us practical advice, based on experience.

I have had a long friendship with a woman I'll call Sandra. From a nutritional standpoint, her home was a disaster. For whatever reasons, her mother virtually never did any cooking, and when she did, she made pancakes or cookies. Sandra and her brothers and sisters snacked on things like crackers and potato chips and cookies and candy and cupcakes. They seldom ate together as a family.

It was every man for himself, and the choices were anything but nutritious.

Sandra had a tough childhood in other respects too. As you can guess, her family's lack of caring about food was reflective of their neglect of their children. Sandra made it through elementary school fairly well, but when adolescence hit, and especially when she entered high school, she really started struggling. Her grades were average, and she felt as though she had to put all her effort into studying, just to get C's. She wrestled with fear and insecurity.

"I looked at all the other kids who had what I wanted and felt so jealous," she told me. "I believed that those other kids 'had it all' and I just didn't, for whatever reason, so there wasn't anything I felt I could do about my situation."

Sandra learned differently when she went to college and rented a room in the home of a family who lived near her school. She was not just a boarder; the family offered her a lot of love and friendship. The woman of the house was also knowledgeable about nutrition and suggested to Sandra that her struggle with mental sluggishness and poor energy might be related to food.

"At first, I didn't like her advice," Sandra told me. "I felt she was meddling in my life, and I didn't want to have to admit that food might be a problem. I finally got so desperate, however, that I began listening to what she was saying, and it started making a lot of sense. I tried a different diet and went to a doctor who agreed that I needed to eat better. I discovered I had been addicted to pancakes and bread and cookies, and that these foods contributed to my sluggishness. After a short time of eating more nutritious foods, I felt noticeably better and had energy I didn't know what to do with. I found that I could think more clearly too."

Sandra's mother had failed to teach her how to make good nutritional choices. She had obviously failed to teach

Sandra to make good emotional and spiritual choices as well. Once Sandra was willing to have a counselor help her deal with the pain and the misinformation that resulted from her neglect, she needed to learn how to identify nourishing choices and how to practice making them. The pathway toward healing and health was open to her through the advice of counselors and friends.

It is important, then, to be reminded that not everything that tastes good is going to be nourishing. Some of it is junk food. Some of it could actually be poisonous. We should know what sources we can trust for good information about nourishment and use them. In other words: get advice. Whether it be parents or friends or a counselor or a minister, talk with a person who seems to be emotionally and spiritually nourished about your life, your work, children, marriage or faith—to get some practical tips about making new choices.

Taste

Even though not everything that tastes good is nourishing, taste should be a factor to consider when we are trying to make decisions. It is amazing how many of us make repeated choices, which are in contrast to who we are and how we feel. Yes, there will be occasions when the reality of life will require us to make a selection that doesn't particularly appeal to us and sometimes that will be for the purpose of nourishing someone else. But we should not get into the habit of denying or ignoring our own hungers or tastes, especially when it comes to the important choices of life, like marriage and career.

· · · · · · · · ·
Career Decisions

Many of us have made decisions about college or vocational school or permanent career choices without regard to whether they are nourishing to us. There is a belief out there in the marketplace that "work" is something you hate for eight hours per day, and that you long for the year you can finally retire. People are making long-term job decisions without consulting their passions.

"Go into computers," many of our young people are told. "It's a growing field with a lot of opportunity."

That's fine, but what if I don't happen to like computers? What if the thought of working in computers is the farthest thing from nourishment that I can think of?

A friend of mine is a popular author, speaker, and expert on choosing jobs and careers. He says that more than seventy percent of the people in the United States are working in jobs that are not well fitted to them and that they don't like. I've heard people express this distress quite often myself. I talked briefly with a man at a holiday dinner several years ago whom I had not seen for several years. When I asked him, "How are you doing?" his reply surprised me.

He said, "Well, only fifteen more years and I can retire." He was serious. He was counting the days and weeks and months to his retirement because he didn't like the work he was doing.

Along the pathway toward our chosen profession, we will all have to work "jobs" that we don't prefer. That's realistic. But the decisions that ultimately lead toward a position that may last for a while are completely on our shoulders. Whether those positions are nourishing to us personally and professionally and financially and spiritually is not something completely out of our control. Despite the winding roads and occasional roadblocks, the pathway can be the result of our choices.

A Man Whose Job Seemed to Be a Roadblock

I love communications and broadcasting, and, I guess, I've always assumed that the people who worked beside me felt the same. One day a co-worker of mine asked if we could get together and talk. I'll call him Bart. He spent nearly thirty minutes telling me about the various problems in his life and how unhappy he was, including being dissatisfied with his job at the radio station. As we talked, I realized that he hadn't really been happy with much of anything.

That was a large problem, which would require more than a short conversation with me, but I decided to try to help him evaluate his choices and make some new ones.

"Tell me, Bart," I asked. "What is the most nourishing thing in your life? What really makes your heart beat with excitement?"

"Sports," he replied. "Sports of any kind. I love them all."

"Have you ever thought about trying to pursue a career in sports?" I asked.

Bart sat for a long time thinking about my question, then he answered, "I guess not. It never occurred to me to try."

"What do you like best about sports?" I continued. "Would you like to be a player?"

"No," he said, "I don't have what it takes to be a professional player. I'd prefer to be on the sidelines, working with the players."

"Have you ever looked into the jobs that are available?" I asked.

"No, I haven't," Bart replied.

Over a period of time, I encouraged Bart to investigate his chances of getting a job with one of the teams; all along he felt it was a useless experiment. Imagine his surprise and delight when he was interviewed by one of the major baseball clubs to work under the team's trainer through a friend's contact with the man. Bart jumped at the chance, and although the first couple of years were difficult because he was the new kid on the block, he eventually moved into exactly the kind of job for which he had dreamed—to work in professional sports alongside the players.

· · · · · · · · ·
Morals and Values

Each of us needs to have some standards, some system of decision-making to help us know when to say "no" to an appetite.

Appetites always say "yes!" That's the job of an appetite.

As I have already described, some of us make the mistake of never consulting our appetites when making decisions; consequently our hunger is seldom satisfied. But there are others who have come to the point of never saying "no" to an appetite, and that can be a serious problem. In fact, it is one of the most crucial questions facing our culture today. Under what circumstances and by what standards do you say "no" to an appetite? There are loud voices that object to making societal decisions based on morals because, they argue, those are "religious" choices. Nowhere is that more apparent than in the confusion over what to tell teenagers about sex. There is widespread recognition of the fact that teens are either having sex or under pressure to have sex and that there are awesome consequences now that go beyond just getting pregnant. There are sexually transmitted diseases which, in some cases, are life altering and incurable and, in other cases, are fatal. We feel the pressure to teach kids to be more *responsible*. There is almost panic, however, if you suggest defining responsibility as saying "no" to sex. Many schools have to be cautious not to insert *moral* perspective into sex education because there is increasing opposition to it. Instead, they are suggesting to teens that the definition of being responsible is to use birth control or to use barriers to sexually transmitted disease or to even choose abortion. In other words, "Don't ever say 'no' to your appetite. That's confining and suffocating. Celebrate life by saying 'yes' to everything." One of the problems I have with these messages is that being sexually active as a teenager is, in itself, an irresponsible choice. Why would we expect those who have demonstrated their irresponsibility in that way to suddenly act responsible by using devices to prevent pregnancy and sexually transmitted diseases?

One of the reasons there is such panic about saying "no" to appetites is that there have been other voices in times past which seem to be saying "don't ever say yes." That, obviously, is just as much of a problem. In a nourished life, there is going to be the celebration of saying "yes" to every hunger God has given us. But in order for it to be truly nourishing, it is going to have to be within the guidelines of knowing when, and why, and how to say "no."

A hamburger may taste good, for example, and the hunger that it satisfies may be natural. If the hamburger has been stolen from someone, however, it is not a nourishing choice. The appetite says "yes," but there is a very good reason for saying "no." That reason is based on morality, a standard which says "that's a wrong thing to do." It is a standard based on concerns which are much larger than a person's appetite. There are times when we say "no" for the good of those around us or for the good of our home or our culture or our country or our world. A person who has developed the habit of always saying "yes" to appetites is a person who has decided that nothing outside of himself is valued more than himself and his hungers.

I am a Christian and believe the Bible is a reliable measuring stick for morals and values. No matter what kind of hunger I may be experiencing or what kind of personal nourishment I think is going to satisfy that hunger, it won't be nourishing if it conflicts with what I have come to respect and trust from the Bible. It makes a lot of sense to base our standards on the God who created us and knows what is or is not going to be nourishing to our lives.

As one person has put it, "He's the one who made us so it makes sense that he's the one who wrote the operations and repair manual." His standards are not designed to unnecessarily restrict the enjoyment and fulfillment of life. To the contrary, they are intended to lead us into the kind of life that we hunger to live.

God's guidelines say to us that, by definition, it is going to be most nourishing to be honest in business, faithful in marriage, considerate in relationships, devoted to God, and responsive to various kinds of needs in the lives of others. There will be other measuring sticks in a particular culture (usually defined by laws) that we may need to be sensitive to as well. The point is that even though we want to make increasing numbers of choices that are nourishing, and we want those choices to appeal to our hungers and our tastes, we cannot be led only by our cravings. Part of the definition of what is ultimately nourishing to us should come from standards outside of ourselves. The most important standards come from God. This means that there are going to be times in our lives when we will have to reject something that would taste good.

Some people may think that they are going to have to live in a world of no pleasure, which doesn't sound very nourishing. The fact is, however, that those who include values and morals in their decisions are the ones who enjoy pleasures the most. They can eat the hamburger without fear or guilt. They can enjoy and explore the depths and the heights of sexual pleasure in a committed, married relationship. Some dimensions of physical satisfaction between two people can only be experienced by those who have been faithful to each other over a long period of time and who have become "partners in pleasure" and co-pilgrims in the living of life. The satisfaction and freedom of making honest money and spending it is worth all the effort of trying to learn the principles and skills of being a productive person in society.

Our own experience, the advice of others, our tastes, and morals and standards—these are the measuring sticks to judge whether or not something that seems good is really nourishing to us. Yet we also need another guideline. Some things may seem to taste sour, but really be good for us in the long run.

· · · · · · · · · ·

Not Everything Nourishing Tastes Good

I guess some would call this the cod liver oil discussion. Very happily, my parents didn't believe in the stuff so I never tasted it. Yet I know a lot of people who were forcibly fed this medicine and many other foul tasting substances as they were told, "This is good for you."

Sometimes the best choice may not appeal to our taste or our definition of what's nourishing, especially if our tastes are too narrow or if we are sick and need something medicinal. Sometimes we are required to consume something unappealing, like cod liver oil, because of its therapeutic value; it's going to give life or promote growth or, in some cases, prevent life from being overtaken by some disease or condition. It is not nourishing to be sick!

I know a man who, as a young person, ate only hot dogs and potato chips. Literally. Why his parents allowed that, I don't know. If someone had put a plate of buttered peas in front of him or offered some freshly sliced peaches, he wouldn't have been interested. If someone tried to convince him that those items were nutritious and that he needed them, he probably would not have accepted that; but even if he had, he would have been faced with the challenge of eating them, even if he didn't like the taste. Finally this man listened to those around him and while in his mid-twenties began to broaden his diet.

The emotional and spiritual side of this is probably clear. There are times when the right choice is not going to be pleasant, or when a painful experience is going to have a nourishing effect on us.

Athletes understand this principle. As I write this, a high school friend of ours is going through what is known as "hell week." He and his team members are getting into condition for the school year. They run until their sides ache, they do calisthenics and smash into one another and chase each other to the point of near exhaustion—and most of this is happening in blistering hot weather. That's nourishing! Yes, for a football player who wants to be in tip-top shape and prepared both physically and mentally to participate in competition.

Failure

Another, not so wonderful, form of nourishment is failure. Most of us fear failure so much, and resist it so intensely, that we don't understand how it could be nourishing. Yet it can be one of the most important aspects of nourishment in our lives. It's easier for us to see that in other people's lives than in our own.

Let's use physical nutrition as an example once again. If someone has been thrust into adulthood from a family that did not teach nourishment, and that person is existing by eating cupcakes and candy bars, one of the most valuable things that could ever happen is to experience some kind of physical crisis, which will make that person face reality and learn something about a proper diet.

Emotional and spiritual failure can lead us to some of the most life-changing and important discoveries, because we then learn to make new choices. No one can expect to live a happy, healthy life without making better choices.

I once spent several weeks asking the Lord to help me understand what factors have contributed to the most powerful and truly permanent changes in my life. During that time I made lists of various things and thought about them in detail. I evaluated radio and television, sermons and books, cassette tapes and teachings, and classes and counselors and family and friends. I wanted to determine which tools had been most effective so I could concentrate on them and make sure I was utilizing them to the best advantage. If books were the answer, I would commit myself to writing. If speakers had been most inspiring in my life, I would devote myself to speaking.

I filled several pages with my observations and evaluations. When I had exhausted the possibilities, I came to one very significant conclusion: The factor that had consistently produced the lasting and vital change in my life was TROUBLE, with a capital "T." All the books and sermons and speakers and counselors had an impact only because I had experienced the kind of pain and failure that made me ready to listen.

Hurting people tend to think that a nourished life is a perfect life, a life without frustration, a life without surprises or loss. When a person like that experiences loss, he or she feels, "I have not yet reached the blissful land in which others around me live." That is a tragic misunderstanding and a fantasy.

I remember when I used to look at other people and think of them as having some magic that I didn't possess, but I haven't often had the experience of somebody thinking of me that way. That happened once when my family and I were on a camping trip. A young man who was camping alone occupied the space next to us at the campground and, over the next several days, we got into some interesting conversations. He was a person who had grown up in a painful home and had struggled through school. He got hooked on drugs and had several encounters with the law and had even spent some time behind bars. After a girl that he loved deeply broke up with him, he was jarred into realizing that he needed to kick his habit. Now, four years later, he was courageously trying to rebuild his life. He told me with pride, "I've registered my car for the first time, and actually purchased insurance for it, as I should have long ago. I'm even learning what it's like to hold a good job."

One day as this young man was returning to his campsite with a bag of ice in his hand, he walked over to where I was seated and said, "You know, you're really lucky. You've got a nice family and a beautiful wife and a job that you like. That's what I want. A wife I can love and kids I can take camping and enough money to do it." The tone of his voice made me feel as if I possessed a fortune.

Even though this young man had lived long enough to know that life is never perfect, he was still looking at me and my family through eyes of fantasy. I knew he imagined that my kids all stood at attention and smiled and said, "Good morning, Father." He thought that my wife and I had an idyllic relationship, and that all I had to do was get out of bed each morning and enough money would have come my way to take my family camping.

I smiled as he described his impression of my life because he didn't know what a winding and pain-filled pathway I had walked. He didn't know about the occasions early in our marriage when Linda and I didn't have enough money to live because of youthful and unrealistic choices I had made and the bitter failures that had helped me to realize them. He didn't know what deep struggles we had had in our personal lives and in our marriage as we had tried to forge a marriage in the midst of the effects of our deep pain. He didn't know how many times I had doubted my professional and spiritual decisions or how many lonely nights I had spent trying to figure out what life is all about.

I tried to tell him all of that, and he sincerely tried to hear, but I still think he went home believing that our family represented something unattainable to him. He didn't know how much some of what he expressed about himself matched how I had sometimes felt about myself.

A nourishing life is not a perfect life; it also includes frustration and surprises and loss, but those can lead us to make better choices.

A Man Who Made a Cod-Liver-Oil Choice

I'll never forget going through a decision of this nature with an acquaintance of mine, Brian, a seminarian who was on the staff of a church in southern California. He once asked if we could get together and talk, and we made an appointment for breakfast at a restaurant near the beach, where we could sit outside and not only talk confidentially but also enjoy the coastline sunshine.

"I'm attracted to a woman from our church who has come to me a few times for counseling," he told me. "I know it's not right and if my wife found out she would be devastated, but I have to be honest and say that I have found caring and understanding and love from this woman that is deeper and better than anything I've ever known."

His story sounded all too familiar. Brian was enjoying their conversations and other intimacies, although he claimed that they had not had a sexual relationship. Their relationship was clearly headed in that direction, however. Brian ultimately decided to end his intimate contact with the woman, and there were two things that helped make up his mind. One was that he concluded that pursuing the relationship would not ultimately be nourishing to anyone. Not to him. Not to the woman. Not to Brian's wife or children. Not to the Lord. Not to his ministry. It was tempting to continue enjoying what he had discovered, but it was unwise and wrong, and he knew it.

The other factor that affected his thinking was the realization that his hunger for nourishment was normal and natural. He didn't have to apologize for wanting to feed that part of himself. The right pathway, however, was to discover why that was not happening between him and his wife and to take steps that would bring it to pass. He felt so helpless in his marriage he thought his relationship with this woman was his only hope, and that if he gave it up, he was relegating himself to a joyless, hopeless existence. As he got into counseling he realized that the hopelessness was because of some of his own pain and that neither his life nor his marriage was at an end. He also came to the jarring realization that he probably would have treated this other woman the same way he was treating his wife and would have eventually felt the same about their relationship if he had married her. Even though cutting off the wrong relationship was difficult and painful and didn't seem immediately nourishing, it was without question the most nourishing decision to make. During the next year Brian and his wife were able to do a lot of work individually and together, which produced the kind of intimacy and friendship he desired. Brian's cod-liver-oil choice turned into a treasure for both of them.

Even the ordeals that seem at the time to be destructive can ultimately lead to nourishment, depending on how we respond to them.

Once again, that depends on our choices. It is ironic how many people have come out of the most devastating of events with some of the most down-to-earth and healthy attitudes about life and the future. Not everything that is nourishing tastes good, and not everything that tastes good is nourishing. Remember that when you're ready to partake of a feast or when you may be forced to take your own dose of cod liver oil. The result might surprise you.

Now That You've Completed the ABCs

In the first part of this book we have been considering the ABCs of nourishment. These principles of nourishment are easy to remember:

- Nourishment begins with yourself.
- You are responsible for your own nourishment.
- Your nourishment should come from more than one source.
- Everything that tastes good is not always nourishing.
- And its corrolary—Everything that is nourishing does not always taste good.

These principles can become yardsticks to measure your relationship with yourself and others. Everyone has a natural desire to nourish themselves and others. Yet so few of us manage to do this. Why is that so? Unfortunately we are often hindered by some unseen obstacles. We'll consider those barriers in Chapter 6.

CHAPTER 6

. . . .

Obstacles
to Nourishment:
Guilt, Fear,
and Perfectionism

One afternoon on "TableTalk" I received a call from a woman who called herself Lorraine. She sounded like a bright, energetic person, and in my mind I saw an image of a woman in her fifties, pleasingly plump, and wearing an apron.

"My mother-in-law lives with us," Lorraine began, "and I really love her, but I've begun thinking thoughts about her that I do not like. I'm even beginning to wish she weren't here."

Lorraine spent quite a bit of time telling me the various things she did for her mother-in-law, such as driving her to the store and to the doctor. She had even quit her job seven years earlier in order to have time to care for her mother-in-law.

"Lorraine," I began, "you have committed yourself in sacrificial ways to your mother-in-law, even to the extent of quitting your job. Now you're feeling guilty that you cannot do more and feel happy about it. I think somebody should throw a banquet in your honor!"

Lorraine chuckled nervously, then began to cry. The person who had been so happy and energetic at the beginning of the call began to show that she was exhausted, angry, and depressed.

"My mother-in-law is such a sweet person," Lorraine sobbed, "and she needs so much help. I just don't want to let her down. She doesn't have anyone else."

"Is she an invalid?"

"Oh, no," Lorraine responded. "She's very healthy."

"Why are you doing so much for her, then?" I asked.

"Well, about seven years ago her husband died, and she didn't take it very well. We were very concerned about her, so my husband and I invited her to come live with us. That's when I quit my job."

"Lorraine, we should all be willing to help anyone, especially a family member, through a tough season. However, I see two problems."

"You do?" Lorraine said, amazed that I should question her charitable attitude.

"First, it sounds to me as if your mother-in-law can do more for herself than you are asking of her. You are going to have to make some choices that will help nudge her to become more independent—for her own good as well as yours.

"The second problem is that even if your mother-in-law needed your care day and night, you would be foolish not to take some time for your own nourishment."

"I think I'm beginning to understand, but I guess I'm still not sure what you mean."

"You have basic needs too, Lorraine. You have the need for rest. That need to interact with your husband and your kids and your special friends. You have the need to get in your car and drive to who-knows-where. In an ironic way, your mother-in-law is better nourished than you are."

"But I don't have time for myself, and I feel guilty if I do take the time."

"That's precisely the problem. Guilt. The kind of guilt that makes it difficult for you to make choices on your own behalf."

Many of us want to nourish ourselves, but feelings of guilt always get in the way of our good intentions.

· · · · · · · · · ·

Obstacles to Nourishment

Hunger is natural. The need to be nourished is natural. So why do we have so much trouble catching on? A lot of obstacles obscure the simplicity of The Nourishment Factor, the easy principle that hunger must be fed by nourishment. No single explanation will apply to every person, but four hindrances are so common and so ubiquitous that most of us can identify with them.

Guilt

One of the biggies we've just mentioned is guilt. I feel guilty and selfish if I make choices for my own nourishment or if I have to say "no" or "not now" to someone in order to nourish myself. Once again let me say that I'm not talking about selfishness, a preoccupation with my own needs at the consistent expense of other people's needs. I'm not saying that we should live our lives for self-nourishment.

I'm arguing that in order to serve others, I have to make sure that I am healthy, which means I must receive the proper nourishment.

It quite literally takes practice to overcome the guilt that prevents us from making nourishing choices or the guilt that comes as we take steps to nourish ourselves.

Two Men Who Were Held Captive by Their Guilt One of my favorite activities is fishing, and one of my favorite spots on the earth for fishing is Canada's beautiful Yukon

Territory. I was introduced to the Far North almost ten years ago when a friend of mine invited me to go with him to the Yukon to do what we smilingly refer to as "conducting a ministry of deliverance on some fish in a lake."

I frequently organize a group of fishermen to go to a particular lodge there, and I've watched a fascinating variety of reactions and emotions as I've talked with people about going. One acquaintance of mine has put in his reservation and deposit nearly every year—and every single time he has ultimately decided not to go. A mountain of guilt is at the root of his struggle. Part of him wants to enjoy a big game fishing trip, but another part of him can't handle the self-centeredness it seems to represent to him, so he sabotages any plans to respond to his hunger for relaxation and enjoyment.

Floyd, a plumber who had a very successful business, did finally go on the trip one year, but not without fighting a heavy battle with guilt. Even after we arrived, he was introspective and quiet, and although he seemed to be having a good time, especially when he hooked into a twenty- or thirty-pound fish, he still seemed preoccupied and sometimes distant.

One day the weather was particularly beautiful on the lake. Floyd and I were sitting in a small boat, which was anchored in what I called "Pike Country," a portion of the lake where we would most likely catch the magnificent great northern Pike, one of the most aggressive game fish.

I thought we were having a great time. Then I looked at Floyd's face, which had the color and expression of rain clouds and thunder rather than reflecting the sunshine and blue skies around us. I asked him straightforwardly if he was having a good time.

"Of course," he replied. "I've never been on a trip like this before. It's a once-in-a-lifetime experience."

I agreed with him. "You don't look as if you feel that way.

Some kind of struggle seems to be going on inside you."

Floyd paused, looked off into space for a moment, then said, "Yes, I am going through a struggle. It's a miracle I came on this trip. I am not the kind of person who does this sort of thing. I dream about hunting and fishing and traveling, and I always say I'm going to do it someday, but I never seem to get around to it. A part of me has really loved being up here in the wilderness and seeing all the beauty. I've even got some great fishing stories to tell when I get back home.

"Another part of me just doesn't feel like I should be here. I guess I'm having a hard time believing that it's okay for me to take time off and have fun. When I'm out here strolling around, I alternate between excitement that I'm really doing this and dread that for some reason I shouldn't be doing it."

"Sounds like industrial strength guilt," I said.

"You're the second person in a week to tell me that," Floyd replied. "My wife thinks it is the result of my upbringing. My dad was the kind of person who worked long hours, seven days a week, and he didn't think much of taking time off. I guess I ended up looking at life the same way he did."

I knew a little about Floyd's background. His father was what we would now call a workaholic and was the model for Floyd's attitude about both work and play. By taking time and money to go fishing with us, and by making a personally nourishing decision, Floyd had violated one of the family doctrines.

In order to nourish ourselves, we need to believe that it is a right thing to do. Guilt will make some of us feel that simple emotional or spiritual nourishment is somehow selfish and inappropriate. Making even the most rudimentary choices of nourishment will be a chore.

You might ask, "How do I overcome that kind of guilt?

How do I start making better and more nourishing choices personally?"

First, just go ahead and make increasing numbers of nourishing decisions. Sometimes it just takes practice and courage to break through a lifetime of accumulated guilt.

Second, realize that frequently some of the intense false guilt in our lives is the result of destruction, usually early in our childhood years. It may require a season of counseling and dealing with the roots of the guilt in order to overcome it.

Fear

Fear and guilt are close cousins. Both are tied to eligibility. By that I mean, each of us expects to receive only what we believe we deserve. This, too, is associated with destruction, like physical, emotional, or sexual abuse or neglect. Many of these people will conclude in a childlike way, "This must have happened because I am eligible for it or else it wouldn't have happened." In the same way there is a childlike conclusion that says, "Since I am eligible for bad stuff to happen, more of it is going to happen. When it does, it is all my fault, because there is just something about me that is eligible for it."

Many of these people are afraid to make self-nourishing decisions because they feel they are stepping outside their limits of eligibility. In other words, it is easy to feel, "I am going to lose. I am going to experience bad things because that's part of my life so I had better not choose very many good things. If I do, I will feel even worse when I lose them." There is also a companion feeling that says, "I had better not experience very many good things, because if I accumulate very many good experiences it will make the bad happen a lot quicker." Fear, then, can stand in the way of my making decisions that are nourishing for my life.

The Day I Couldn't Win   A story from my own childhood illustrates what I'm talking about. As a child I developed a friendship with a man whom many of us kids considered to be a celebrity. He was a child evangelist and had been well known in his day. Much to my delight, he decided to retire in the city where I lived and to take over the junior church responsibilities at the church my father pastored. He was an enchanting character who did magic tricks and told captivating stories and gave everyone small, but unique, gifts at the end of every service.

Once he announced that there was going to be a contest, and that the winner of the contest would get to make the first choice from among a group of prizes. Each week the awards were lined up in front of the junior church for all of us to see. Everyone's eye was on the biggest and the best prize: a beautiful, huge cuckoo clock with a Swiss boy and girl who danced around a platform on the top of the clock, every hour on the hour.

We could do various things to earn points to win this coveted prize, such as inviting neighborhood friends to junior church or memorizing Bible verses. I worked hard to make certain I came out on top. Emotionally, however, I faced a predicament. On one hand, I wanted to win and I wanted that cuckoo clock. On the other hand, I had such a wounded view of myself from my early years I couldn't handle it if I did win. I was actually afraid to win. Winning was inconsistent with my basic view of myself. I did not understand why.

The big day came when the contest reached its conclusion. The retired evangelist announced the winning names with the fanfare reserved for such an event. Much to my combined delight and torment, I came out on top! As I was called to the front of the room along with the two kids who had come in second and third, I knew that I was going to have the opportunity to choose the cuckoo clock. Yet I was overcome with dreadful fear. Almost as if I were watching a slow motion movie, I saw myself bypass the cuckoo clock. Instead I chose a nondescript candleholder, which was sitting next to the coveted clock. The candleholder was the stupidest object on the prize table.

All the kids in the room were shocked, especially the girl who had come in second. She quickly ran over to claim the cuckoo clock. The junior church pastor stood in silence for the longest time as though he was trying to comprehend what had just happened and whether he should do anything to try to change it. It was a horrible moment for me.

Because of some of the debris in my own life, I had come to the conclusion that I wasn't eligible for something as nice as the cuckoo clock, and I couldn't bring myself to choose it, especially in front of all those other kids. I sabotaged my own prize! I somehow felt that it was going to be more "proper" for me to let one of the other contest winners choose it.

It was many years before I could look upon that experience with more understanding of what it meant and why I had chosen the way I did.

Perfectionism

This is another biggie. Some of us feel that everything has to be finished—and finished perfectly—before we can make a choice that is nourishing to us.

Yet a principle of nourishment is: *Nourishment occurs in the midst of that which is unfinished, imperfect, and flawed.* What would you think of a person who would never eat breakfast, lunch, or dinner until everything in the house—or in that person's life or family—was perfect?

Some of us want the entire world to be organized before an important dinner or a special event, but many of us have learned the important reality that good things can occur in the middle of whatever is going on, whether it is finished or perfect or clean or organized or controlled—or not. Unfortunately some people postpone emotional and spiritual decisions of nourishment, because they feel that "someday" the conditions in their lives will finally be right. "Then I can enjoy a vacation or an evening out," they think.

Hogwash!

A lot of us need to practice making nourishing choices in the midst of whatever is going on. Life is never totally under control. About the time we get our houses looking perfect there's an earthquake or a tornado or an illness. When we finally feel as if we've gotten all our work caught up, there is a war in the Middle East and our son is called to active duty. There is never—let me repeat, *never*—a "perfect" time to wait to make nourishing choices. We do not wait for the "perfect" time to eat, and we should not wait for the perfect time to receive emotional and spiritual nourishment.

David, a Man Who Knew How to Make the Proper Choices I've enjoyed a friendship of several years with an attorney whose ability to make good choices has been an inspiration to me. David is one of the busiest people I know. He has the responsibility of a law firm with numerous clients, a large family, and several volunteer or charitable commitments. And he occasionally suffers from a medical condition that causes him a lot of pain. Through the years I have watched him blend his responsibilities and his pain with nourishment for himself, his family, and others. When a special vacation or a fishing trip looms on the horizon, he's not saying to himself, *In order to really be eligible for this, I have to have everything done and all of my life organized*. He simply inserts the nourishment into the middle of whatever is going on at the time, whether that's a peaceful moment or a chaotic one.

A Lady Who Practices What She Preaches This principle is also true when we are nourishing others. I have appreciated the life and some of the writings of Edith Schaeffer, wife of evangelical theologian Francis Schaeffer. In one of her books she talks about the importance of taking time in the middle of whatever is going on to nourish those who are around us, especially children. When childrearing years are over, she says, you'll forget a lot of occasions of mopping the floor or doing the dishes, but you'll cherish the times you stopped working to hear something your child wanted to say. That is not to say that children should rule the day. It is important for children to learn to respect other people's boundaries. But most of us would have to admit that many of the times we have said "no" to our children, we would have been wiser to have helped them with their needs.

I've had the privilege of visiting with Edith Schaeffer more than once. During one of our talks she demonstrated to me that she meant what she had written about seizing those little moments to nourish others in the midst of a hectic life. We had just finished doing a one-hour interview about a new book she had written, and she was on a tight schedule. In fact, she was to leave the radio station and drive to Palm Springs where she was going to be spending time with an internationally known woman. Her companion, and driver, was urging her to hurry, but she took a moment before she left the studio to sign a copy of her book, and she did it in a surprising way. She didn't just quickly scribble her name. She spent time actually drawing a picture in the book, a scene with mountains and flying birds, and then she inscribed a personal message. I protested, saying that she was in a hurry and didn't have to do all that. She smilingly scolded me and said she wanted to do it because she was making the most of the short time we had to talk. She is known for making people feel they are more important to her at that moment than anything— or anyone—else.

Edith Schaeffer knows how to nourish herself and others. She doesn't wait for the perfect moment. She makes the little moments count. We'll talk more about nourishing others in Part 3.

PART 3

Nourishing Other People

C H A P T E R 7

. . . .
Nourishing
Others

Now we're going to get to what some of you have been waiting for—nourishing others.

Let me repeat, however, that it is important to talk about personal nourishment first because that's where it all begins. To make sure that you have the strength for all the other commitments that are important to you is not selfish, and many of us have had the impression that it is.

At this point, then, let me loudly proclaim that one of the important principles of nourishment is the nourishment of those around us. A nourishing life is a life that is nourishing to others. A selfish life is a life that is not nourishing to others or a life that is seeking our own nourishment to the destruction of others.

One of the most fulfilling experiences of life is to offer nourishment to those who are around us, especially to those who mean the most to us. Whether we are feeding a starving stranger or offering a cup of tea to an otherwise well-nourished friend, there is a warmth exchanged and a feeling of having contributed to that person's well-being.

At first thought, it might not seem necessary to talk very much about nourishing others because it is such a satisfying and simple thing to do. We usually say, "If you spot someone who is hungry, feed him!"

Unfortunately, it is not as easy as that. In order to have a truly nourishing impact on others, we need to discuss some of the factors that can help us do it best.

· · · · · · · · ·
Feeding Those Who Are Hungry

The fact is, folks, that some of us have a hunger to feed other people whether they want to be fed or not. And that's not nourishing!

We need to be sensitive to the other person's needs and hungers as a part of trying to decide if we should respond and what form that response should take.

As some of you may have heard, my wife and I have a houseful of children—seven at last count. We've gone through childbirth a bunch of times. I've always appreciated how much people want to be of help to us when a new baby arrives. They offer to take care of the other kids while Mom is recuperating, or they suggest they can bring meals for a few days, or they volunteer to help clean the house. Those offers are deeply appreciated. On a couple of occasions, however, individuals have invaded our home and our lives whether we wanted them there or not, and the results were anything but nourishing.

The Lady Who Had to Volunteer I remember one time when we were expecting our sixth child, and we had everything planned for the days following the birth (after all, we were old pros by that time!). We had arranged for friends or family to help where needed, and I had made plans to take time off from my ministry schedule to run things at home. I love to cook and do quite a bit of the cooking in our home, so I had the meals completely under control.

Shortly after the baby was born, I received a call from an acquaintance of ours, a lady who was filled to overflowing with energy and enthusiasm and who had a reputation for ambushing my wife or me either at the front door or over the phone with seemingly endless conversation. She was a very sincere person and was an untiring and unselfish volunteer, but she didn't know when to stop herself.

"This is Stella Larson calling," she began. "I'm calling to let you know that I have made dinner for your family this evening, and I'll be bringing it over in an hour."

"That's very nice of you," I replied, "but we really haven't needed any help with meals, and, in fact, I'm about to prepare our evening meal myself."

"Well, don't you worry yourself about it," Stella continued, "because I want to help you and your sweet wife."

"It's no problem at all," I assured her. "I thoroughly enjoy cooking. I really do appreciate your thinking of us, but everything's under control."

"But it's all done!" she protested. "All I have to do is drop by the store and get some bread and drive to your house. It'll just take a jiffy."

I was beginning to get irritated by her insistence, but I also realized she apparently had a kitchen full of food that she had spent time preparing for us. So I decided to find out what was on the menu. "What did you fix?" I asked.

"Cream of mushroom chicken casserole," she said, "with French bread to stick in the oven."

Oh joy! I thought to myself. *My kids will not touch that under threat of death.* "Listen, Stella," I said out loud. "I appreciate your offer, and I'm sorry you've gone to all this trouble to put together a meal for us, but I'm telling you that we're doing okay. I feel bad about this, but my kids are not into mushrooms. Some of them even conduct major investigations to find out what is hidden in casseroles."

There was an uncomfortable pause on the phone, then Stella abruptly said, "I'm bringing over the food. I'll see you."

Sure enough, Stella showed up at the front door about forty minutes later with a hot casserole dish and a bag full of other goodies to go along with it. I had little choice but to thank her for it and promise to give back the casserole dish. I closed the door and stood there for a minute, holding a dinner in my hands that would have to be given to someone else to keep from going to waste, with a feeling of having been intruded upon by someone who was actually trying to help.

Stella didn't realize it, but she was the kind of person who ran all over other people because of her own hunger to feel needed. If she truly were concerned for my family, she would have phoned to find out what we might need so she would know how she might help us.

So to nourish others, *we need to be sensitive to their true needs for nourishment so we don't end up in the awkward position of feeding someone who is not hungry.*

This experience also offers a good example of proper boundaries. I had a boundary that said, "I don't want my family invaded, and, besides, I have chosen to offer physical nourishment to them tonight myself." Stella was the kind of person who had demonstrated on prior occasions that she either didn't notice other people's boundaries and territories, or she didn't really care about them. All she cared about was her desire to "nourish" someone else, whether it was truly nourishing or not. For her, boundaries were either to be ignored or battered. She offered a particularly difficult challenge to my boundaries. After that experience, I never allowed her to do it again— for any reason.

I might add, out of fairness to Stella, two or three years later she came to me at the end of a church service, in which I had spoken, and apologized for some of the things that had happened. I appreciated that, and it thawed some of the awkwardness between us. After that I allowed her to penetrate our boundaries a couple of times without having to be as uptight about what was going to happen.

· · · · · · · · · ·

Let Others Carry Responsibility for Their Own Nourishment

If you're faced with a stranger who is hungry or a friend who needs money or a relative who needs a place to live, it's difficult to decide if helping them is going to be nourishing or if it might be counterproductive.

One afternoon on "TableTalk" I received a call from a listener who identified herself as Irene. "My daughter, Sherry, is twenty-six years old," she began, "and wants to live at home while she completes college. I don't know whether to let her do it or not. I'm getting kind of tired of having her here."

Irene and I chatted for a few minutes so I could get a better picture of Sherry. I soon realized that she had never made a serious attempt to go to college and had been living at the continuous expense of her parents.

"Your daughter is an adult," I told Irene. "She needs to carry that responsibility. As long as you pay for her car and her insurance and give her fun money, why should she live anywhere else but home? She's never shown any interest in college before you insisted that she move out, and now she's playing on your heart strings so you will keep giving her your family's version of welfare."

"But she's my daughter!" Irene moaned. "I should help her as much as I can."

"I agree," I replied. "But you need to choose the kind of

help you offer so it will be healthy and productive, not unhealthy and counterproductive."

"I guess I'm just confused about which is which," Irene sighed. "I don't want to cut her off altogether."

"Let's use the illustration of physical nourishment," I suggested. "When Sherry was born, she was totally dependent on you for nourishment, right?"

"Right," Irene agreed.

"As she grew, however, you handed more and more of the responsibility for her nourishment over to her. She learned to use her own spoon for breakfast cereal, then she learned to butter her own toast, then she learned to fry her own breakfast eggs, and finally she learned to make a hamburger. Now she's an adult and she has the responsibility to take care of herself, as all adults do.

"She should be carrying the burden for planning her own meals, earning money to buy the food for those meals, and learning what those meals should consist of so she can be truly nourished."

"I agree with that," Irene replied.

"The same principle is true about other areas of her life as well, Irene," I said. "Sherry should be responsible for earning money, finding a place to live, deciding whether to go to college, owning a car, choosing her friends, contemplating marriage, learning how to live in the world. You can give her any advice she will accept, and you can pray for her and encourage her, but it will be wrong for you to actually carry the responsibility for her. If she is going to go to college, she needs to be the one to get the forms and submit them to the college. She needs to inquire about scholarships and campus housing. She needs to put work and thought into a career, instead of you and your husband doing it for her.

"Right now you are treating her as if she were a baby," I continued. "It's as if you are putting her into a high chair at the age of twenty-six and spoon-feeding her baby food. No parent would ever do that, and yet from an emotional standpoint that's what's happening."

"But does that mean I don't ever help her?" Irene asked.

"It doesn't mean that at all," I answered. "Let me use the nourishment analogy again. Just because you have stopped carrying personal responsibility for your daughter's eating doesn't mean that you stop nourishing her. It only means you stop carrying the responsibility that she should carry for herself. If she is a responsible person, you still invite her over for dinner from time to time or invite her to a restaurant. You still might give her gifts of food on some occasions. You don't completely stop offering her anything to eat. You just resign from the responsibility of having to make decisions for her at the expense of making those choices herself.

Codependency

One of the buzzwords right now among people who are trying to overcome pain and torment in their lives is *codependency*. That's really what I've been describing. A good way to understand codependency is to picture the twenty-six-year-old in the high chair. When we carry responsibility for another person, which that person ought to be carrying personally, we are involved in a smothering, binding, unhealthy relationship with that person, which prevents him or her from carrying the responsibility to deal with life.

Picture what often happens in the life of an alcoholic. That alcoholic needs to carry total responsibility for his addiction and the consequences of that addiction. It is easy for his wife, however, and other family members too, to share in carrying that responsibility. His wife may deny the seriousness of the problem or cover up for his alcoholism. She may hide her husband's addiction from the children or lie for him when he can't go to work or has done something regrettable because of his drinking. When he starts to feel the pain of his condition, it will be tempting for her to try to ease his pain.

The wife may think this is the loving, committed thing to do, but it actually results in her becoming a part of his addiction. He may as well be lying in a baby crib, wearing a diaper, and sucking his thumb, because people are protecting him from having to face the brutal reality of his problem. Once family members realize their own codependency, however, they start letting the consequences rest on the alcoholic's shoulders.

That is when the wife says, "I love my husband, but I'm not going to lie for him anymore. I'm not going to ease the pain of being arrested for drunk driving anymore. I'm not going to shield the reality of his problem from the family anymore. I'm not going to avoid getting help for me and my family anymore."

If one of your choices is to help an addicted person or an irresponsible person to avoid personal responsibility for his or her own life and conduct, you are a part of that person's problem.

Even though the wife of an alcoholic may make the courageous commitment to stop carrying responsibility for her husband's problem and to let him carry the load, she will still nourish him in other, healthy manners such as honoring the things about her husband that are good or noble and being sensitive to some of his needs. She is no longer going to confuse those appropriate responses to him, however, with codependency. She's not going to interfere with the requirement for him to be personally, and solely, accountable for his own conduct and nourishment.

· · · · · · · · ·

Exchanging Nourishment

Ideally, any relationship is going to be one in which there is a mutual sharing of nourishment. This may not be totally balanced every minute of every day because each of you will go through differing seasons of need, but over a period of time the nourishment should be mutual.

It is important in friendships, for example, to ask, "Is this relationship committed only to the needs of one person?" It is very easy for some of us to agree to friendships that are essentially lopsided.

I frequently receive calls from people who are hungry for friendship and who feel that they cannot have friends. They describe how they have attended various churches or clubs and have been ignored by others. They are very angry about that. Frankly, most of the time these people need to get good counseling to deal with some very deep hurts which are hindering them from establishing friendships. Often people who have an enormous hunger from years of not being nourished will walk into a group and require either the group or someone within the group to fill that hunger.

You need to be careful if you tend to be like that because the intensity of your hunger can overwhelm those whom you want to befriend and also blind you to the fact that in order to receive nourishment in a friendship, you need to be able to offer nourishment as well.

I once befriended a young man I'll call Bill, a recluse who had been brought to the church where I was pastoring by a young couple who felt sorry for him. I could write an entire book about the experiences we had with Bill over the next four or five years. He was one of the most complex and fascinating people I've ever met.

If you had seen him sitting and sulking at the rear of the church on Sunday mornings, you would have wondered if he were a street person who had wandered in from Skid Row. He always wore dark glasses and wrinkled clothes. Sometimes there was such a look of hate on his face that I could imagine him pulling a gun in the middle of a service and blasting away at anybody in range.

As I got to know Bill, however, I realized he was a very

intelligent, if not brilliant, person who had grown up under circumstances that never allowed him to discover how smart he really was. One of the issues he grappled with was friendship. He had attended a fellowship for single adults but was turned off by what he called "their judgmentalism." As I questioned him about that I realized that he was walking into the single adult meetings with an attitude that said, "Here I am. Come welcome me. Come meet me. Come establish friendship with me." He didn't see the picture others saw of himself—a moping figure, hiding in the corner without moving in any way, except to glance furtively around the room. Bill could look downright strange.

"Bill, you could be visiting a group of people who need nourishment as badly as you," I suggested, "but you are acting as though the only concern any of them should have is to discern and meet your needs. You don't have to apologize for your needs, and I believe that God wants you to have the kind of friendships in which your needs will be met. That's not likely to happen, however, until you start thinking of nourishing others, rather than just thinking of yourself."

"I guess I don't know how to do that," he admitted.

"Next time you go to a meeting," I suggested, "try to ask yourself, 'What can I do to offer nourishment to these people, rather than just demanding it for myself?' Most people are going to respond to someone who seems to care about them, and that, of course, will be nourishing to you too."

"But how do I do that?" he asked. "How am I going to be friendly to someone I've never met before?"

"Think about it for a while," I told him. "What do you need as you walk into the meeting? What would be nourishing to you? That's a good place to begin in trying to nourish someone else."

We ultimately concluded that a very basic way to offer

simple nourishment to a stranger is to give that person the opportunity to talk about himself or herself. Bill actually memorized a list of ten questions that he could use to start a conversation with another person.

It seemed like a small step, but for Bill it was life-changing. He attended the next meeting with three goals: to get the name of every person there, to find out what country or state each person considered to be home, to learn what kind of job or career each had. The act of offering nourishment, instead of demanding it, produced more that was nourishing for him than he had ever experienced.

I might add that Bill went on to make several friends in that group, including a young woman who eventually became his wife.

What About Those Who Always Seem to Be in Need?

One of the most difficult decisions about nourishing others occurs when someone seems to be repeatedly in trouble or habitually in need, whether that someone is a panhandler on the street or a relative who never seems to have a job. Again The Nourishment Factor can help us to make this decision. Our goal is to either require that the chronically needy person carry the responsibility for his or her own nourishment or to help nudge that person in the right direction.

I have had to put a lot of thought into this problem because as a Christian I know that I am supposed to be responsive to those who have needs. I remember a caller to my program who was struggling with the same issue. She called herself Janet.

"There is a man who has been hanging around our neighborhood for several days," Janet shared. "He is homeless, I know, because he sleeps in a small park near our home, and during the day he just wanders around or sits on a bench in the park. I have really felt sorry for him and have sent sandwiches to him a couple of times through the kids.

"This afternoon I felt so sorry for him that I actually walked over to the park, talked with him myself, and invited him to our house for dinner. He accepted the invitation and immediately came to the house with me, but when my husband got home a couple of hours later, he threw the guy out. I'm crushed, Rich, because this man is lonely and hungry and was probably looking forward to a good, hot meal."

"Did you wonder if it was safe for you and the kids to have this man in your home?" I asked.

"Of course," she replied, "but if I turned down every stranger that comes to my door, I'd never help anyone," she reasoned.

"Janet," I answered, "it is right for your heart to say 'yes' to this man or anyone else like him. I believe Christ wants us to notice the poor and the homeless and to respond to their need. But there are times when other factors might say 'no.'"

"Like what?" she asked.

"Like wisdom," I replied. "Even though your heart said 'yes' to this wandering man, wisdom would probably say 'no' to inviting him into your home. There are other, much wiser ways to help this man."

"Like what?" Janet asked again.

"Well, you could have waited until your husband got home to discuss what ought to be done with him, for instance. From there, you could have looked into your community to see if there is a shelter or a church program that is prepared to professionally respond to a man like this. You could have offered to either take him there or to have someone pick him up. You could even offer to help pay for some of his initial expenses in a shelter, including food."

"I guess I never thought of that," Janet responded. "I

really did take a chance, but I thought it was the right thing to do."

I have often struggled with this problem myself. Once, when I was on the staff of a church that was located just off a major highway, between two major cities, a lot of drifters who were coming through town stopped at the church. We also happened to be the first church listed alphabetically in the telephone book so we got most of the initial telephone calls from people looking for help. I got a real education as I heard all the stories people would tell about why they were begging for food or a few dollars. I wanted to make right decisions about them, and at first I would invest a lot of time trying to decide if their stories were really true. I'd sometimes even call people in other states to try to verify a particular story. During that time I developed a strategy for helping street people, which has been a part of my life ever since.

First, I equipped myself, as best as I could, to give service and goods rather than money. If a man claimed he wanted groceries, I had a storage room filled with food. If a person claimed he needed gas, I had an arrangement with a local gas station to provide it. If a person was desperate for food, I had coupons that were good at a local restaurant for a chicken dinner.

Later we decided that we would give money too, but under certain specific guidelines:

If a drifter called the church and asked for help, we would try to match our help to his need as much as possible. If he claimed he needed money, our policy was to give up to $25 with no qualifications and no questions asked. The drifter didn't need to tell a long complicated story, and he didn't need to try to justify the gift in any way. I would interrupt the stories (many of which were not true anyway) and tell the drifter that this money was God's money and was being given to him in the name of Jesus Christ. He didn't have to explain to me why he needed the money or what he was going to do with it. That, I explained, was between him and God. He was not accountable to me. He was accountable to God. If he used the money for food or gas or lodging, that was great. If he used it for something else, such as drinking or drugs, that was his problem and was between him and God.

This request from any person would be honored once with no strings attached. If the same person popped up again looking for money or food, however, we sat down with him and explained that our continued help was available, but only on one condition—that he would submit to counseling, attend at least one of our ministry events at the church (such as morning or evening or midweek service), and be willing to do some minor amount of work around the church.

If that person was ready to take a small step toward carrying responsibility for his own nourishment, our simple requests would be agreeable to him. If not, he'd disappear. It was a simple test of how much of his own load he was willing to carry.

These principles work well with people whom we know such as friends and relatives. Sometimes wisdom says "no." Sometimes your pocketbook says "no." If a relative of mine who is habitually out of work wants my help, I'll give a modest amount of help with no questions asked— the first time. After that, my help is going to have some strings attached. If I feel that person needs professional counseling, for example, and if that person is willing to receive it, I might be willing to help financially for a short time. My strategy would be to help that person take a step that could ultimately result in his carrying responsibility for his own life again.

It's surprising how often somebody comes to you with a desperate need, and then refuses your help if there is a string attached which requires him or her to carry any measure of responsibility. There are going to be a lot of other occasions, however, when wisdom or practicality or some other good reason will prompt me to say "no" even though my heart says "yes."

· · · · · · · · ·
The Guilt Connection

Some of us don't realize when we're helping another person in an unhealthy way. Others do, but help those people anyway. Why do we repeatedly give money to a person who is irresponsible or allow someone who is undependable to continue living in our home?

Very often it is because of a factor I have already discussed and which I call "The Guilt Connection." In other words, we feel guilty if we turn somebody down. In some cases we also feel that saying "no" would be selfish. The Nourishment Factor can help us make a more objective decision, which is not as colored by our guilt.

I recently received a call from a woman who called herself George, a name many women use when calling my program in order to remain anonymous.

"I'm really frustrated about my sister," she began. "About four years ago she moved in with my mom, and it's beginning to look like she isn't ever going to leave."

"How old is your sister?" I asked.

"She's thirty-six."

"How does your mom feel about your sister being there?" I continued.

"She wants her to get out on her own," George replied. "They don't always get along, and my sister is taking financial advantage of my mom. It's all turned into a big mess. My sister does not have a job and depends on my mom for money. My mom has a good job, but she is getting near retirement age, and I'm afraid she's not going to have any money left when she does retire. I need to know what I can say to my sister to get her to stop this."

"Has your mother told her to leave?"

"My sister knows that Mom doesn't like having her there. All they do is fight."

"But has your mother actually looked her in the eye and told her that it's time to move on?" I asked.

"Well, not exactly, but I've told my sister that she needs to get out."

"What you're describing tells me a lot about your family," I told George.

"Like what?"

"That you've all been through enormous pain."

"Yeah, that's right," George answered. "My father was an alcoholic, and we really went through hell. He and my mom divorced about twenty years ago."

"The reason I know that," I continued, "is that those of us who have experienced the destruction of abusive relationships tend to have a feeling that we are personally responsible for all hurting people who come our way, especially if they are a part of the family."

"Why is that?" George asked.

"There are a number of reasons," I answered, "but one of the biggest is that as a child I feel that I am the center of the world, and everything that happens in that world means something about me. If I experience pain and loss, I tend to think that it is because I am eligible for it, and that it means something horrible about me. I actually start feeling that if anything goes wrong in my world, it is my fault and therefore my responsibility to fix it.

"I once talked with a lady in southern California who actually feared that she was the cause of a big earthquake in 1971. She was a victim and had the tendency to think that everything that happened was somehow because of her.

"You and your mother and your sister are each swimming in guilt," I continued. "You feel personally responsible for much of what happens in each other's lives and would feel personal blame if anything distressing happened."

"But I love my mother and my sister. I can't just sit and watch them kill each other."

"If anyone was truly going to get killed, you'd be right. We do have to intervene in a dramatic way if anyone's life is in danger. But nobody's really going to die in this situation. They just can't live together. And the three of you can't let one another carry responsibility for the others."

"I guess I don't understand," George replied.

"Your mother is not treating her like a thirty-six-year-old. She's treating her like a six-year-old. Mom cannot let your sister bear responsibility for herself. She gives her money, a place to live, and who knows what other favors."

"Like loaning her the car all the time," George interjected.

"Exactly," I agreed. "But notice something else that's going on. When Mom gets fed up with this, what does she do? She calls you. And what do you do? You start carrying Mom's responsibility to try to do something about your sister. In an interesting way, you're doing something similar with your mom to what your mom is doing with your sister."

"What should I do?" George asked.

"The same thing your mother should do," I replied. "Let the adult bear the burden of handling these decisions. In the same way that your sister needs to be required to take her own steps, your mom does too. That doesn't mean anybody abandons anybody. When your mom calls, listen to her, sympathize with her, and give her your advice, if she'll take it. But let the duty of actually handling it rest on her shoulders. The only exception to that would be if, for some reason, she were impaired and simply should not be expected to handle such a task."

"I shouldn't talk to my sister about moving out of Mom's house?" George asked.

"That's up to you. You can have any discussions with her you think would be successful. The problem is when you assume responsibility that should be your mom's, not only is an extra burden added to your shoulders, your mom doesn't have to make the difficult decisions that she needs to make. And your sister's problem grows worse because she has come to realize that Mom's never going to effectively require her to do anything."

"I always thought that talking with my sister for my mom was a way of showing my love."

"You don't have to apologize for your love," I replied. "That's the right kind of connection, what I call The Love Connection. It prompts us to make caring and healthy decisions for one another. The other connection, The Guilt Connection, causes us to make sincere but sometimes destructive decisions for one another."

CHAPTER 8

. . . .

Nourishing
Your
Marriage

I was once invited to speak at a small church in the mountains of northern California. It was such a beautiful town that you would think everybody there was well-nourished just from living there! I had a wonderful time meeting the people at the church and ministering to them and was then introduced to a couple in whose home I would be staying that night. Jim and Terri were nearly forty and had two children. He was an executive with the local power company, and she was a teacher at the beautiful little school located in the middle of town.

As we traveled the mountain road to their home, I was enjoying the scenery and the quiet surroundings and, frankly, was wishing that I could move my family to such a lovely spot. I imagined myself owning a small piece of property with a fish pond and horses and lots of room for the kids to experience "the country."

Jim and Terri's home was stunning. They had purchased an old farmhouse, a dignified white frame, which was decorated with antiques. My room looked like something from *Little House on the Prairie,* complete with a small wood-burning stove in the corner.

I didn't know it at first, and Jim and Terri had certainly not planned it, but my visit had come in the middle of a whopping storm in their marriage. It didn't take long after we had arrived at their home to notice that all was not well. Terri was trying to be polite and gracious, but she looked as if she were going to cry. Jim was doing his best to play the role of a host, but he was clearly angry and impatient with Terri.

· · · · · · · · · ·
Nourishment in Marriage

A marriage is something real and living and, like anything alive, it needs nourishment to stay alive.

It's interesting, however, that some people who would never forget to feed their dog or their cat haven't fed their marriage for months, or even years. I have sat across the counseling desk from countless couples who are disappointed in and angry with each other. Their marriages are gasping for life, but they are not considering nourishing their relationships, even though they are contemplating divorce. I have gone through painful and difficult seasons in my own life and marriage. These times were followed by the jarring realization that it had been a long time since true nourishment had been consciously exchanged. It is as though we expect our marriages to exist forever without having to nourish them in conscious ways.

If you evaluate many marriages, it becomes clear that there are stages of nourishment in a love relationship. Think back to the days when you were madly in love with the person who became your spouse. There was a deep hunger in both of your hearts and a dedication to feeding that hunger in sometimes lavish ways. Most couples in love are pictures of generous and sometimes extravagant nourishment. They spend enormous amounts of time together. It doesn't matter what they are doing as long as they are together. Telephone calls will sometimes cost more than a good meal, but they don't mind as long as they are hearing each other's voices. If they are separated by distance, no problem. One or the other will drive all night just to steal a few moments together. Gifts, both big and small, nourish each other. There seems to be no end to the creative ways that they can find to encourage or to lift each other. If there are shortcomings, they are easily overlooked. If there are bad times, they can be endured. If they are broke, it doesn't seem to matter because they can shower one another with lots of wonderfully nourishing love.

For varying reasons, this exuberant attention starts falling off after marriage. They settle into the daily grind. The intoxication of love wears off and problems that were obscure or covered up become visible and irritating. Much of the change in their relationship occurs because they have become so busy, especially after children come into the picture. Even partners who want to continue nourishing one another in generous ways find it is not always possible because of the demands of life.

The time comes, then, when two ebullient nourishers who were overfeeding one another on a regular basis become two starving people, like Jim and Terri, who resent each other for not providing the nourishment each wants and needs.

Answers to human problems are not easy so I'm not going to suggest that there is a magic answer for every marriage. Each marriage in distress needs a good diagnosis to know what needs to be done next, but in general I think we would all agree that all couples, especially those whose marriages are going through problems, need to evaluate whether any nourishing is going on.

Sometimes what I find are two people who have been in love, who want to be loved and loving, who want a happy marriage . . . but who are starving to death emotionally and spiritually and who deeply resent the other person for not recognizing and responding to that hunger. Each of them has understandable hurt and anger but, in their own starvation, cannot see that the other person is starving too.

Jim and Terri were an example of two people caught together in hurt and anger, each unable to notice the other's misery. Chuck and Melinda were another classic example.

They had been married for almost twenty years, had three children, a commitment to the Lord and a fairly prosperous life-style.

After years of built-up emotions, however, there was finally an explosion. Melinda, who felt that Chuck had never really understood her needs, fell apart. She didn't want to continue with her job as a teacher, she stopped being sexually responsive to Chuck, she began making what Chuck thought were bizarre choices such as buying expensive Persian rugs for the house when she had never seemed to have an interest in them before. During that time, Chuck developed an inappropriate closeness with a woman at work which, although it never blossomed into an affair, could be described as "an affair of the heart."

In the middle of this, I received calls from both Chuck and Melinda.

"Chuck is treating me hatefully," Melinda cried. "All I'm asking for is a little tenderness and understanding, but every time we try to talk about it, he goes into a tirade about what a terrible wife I am."

"Melinda is going crazy," Chuck complained. "She claims that she wants me to be a better husband, but every time I try to get close to her, she pushes me away. I don't know what she wants."

Chuck and I spent a couple of hours one afternoon talking about it all while sitting on the end of a fishing pier off the coast of southern California.

"Melinda is starving to death emotionally," I told Chuck. "I don't endorse her actions and a lot of what she is saying and doing is destructive, but if you don't recognize that it is because of her starvation and her hurt, you're going to lose her . . ."

"Last week," Chuck interjected, "she spent an entire day shopping for these Persian rugs she's become so infatuated with, and brought home two of them that we can't afford. In addition to that, I think they're ugly. I don't like them. Then when she does come home and I try to tell her not to spend so much money on this stuff, she starts crying and telling me what a rotten husband I am and how I'm trying to control her life. I'm getting tired of it."

"Chuck," I said, "you are absolutely right that her preoccupation with the rugs is unhealthy and that spending money you don't have on them is wrong. It's going to be important, however, for you to see why she's acting that way, to see the fact that she is literally starving emotionally."

Chuck still didn't want to see that.

"Let me use an example," I suggested. "Let's imagine there was a person in your family who was caught stealing food from a supermarket. That would be wrong, wouldn't it?"

"Of course," Chuck replied.

"Anyone would be justified to condemn the stealing of food," I continued, "and the person stealing it would have to bear responsibility for doing it."

Chuck nodded in agreement.

"Even though the stealing is wrong and it shouldn't happen, it would be a significant discovery if you found that the person stealing it hadn't had anything to eat for several weeks. That still doesn't justify it, but it does explain it."

I paused to let that sink in.

"Chuck," I said gently, "Melinda is acting the way she is because she is hurting. She is starving for nourishment and more than that, she's starving for nourishment from you."

"But I do love her," Chuck said with tears in his eyes. "I don't know what she wants. I've been faithful to her and provided for her. There isn't anything I wouldn't do for her."

"You know what Chuck," I answered. "I know you mean that and I know it's true. You have provided and you have tried to be faithful. But how do you nourish her emotionally?"

There was a long pause. Finally, Chuck said, "I guess I don't."

We talked about it for quite a while and Chuck realized that he had never been emotionally nourished by his parents so he didn't know how to nourish his wife or his children emotionally. "I guess I've known that," Chuck admitted. "But I resented the fact that Melinda seemed to ignore all the other good things that I've done for her. I thought she was being ungrateful."

It took a while for both Chuck and Melinda to work through their problems, but one of the most important issues was nourishment. Melinda was starving; therefore, she didn't have any emotional energy for responding to Chuck in the ways that he needed, such as sexually, so he began to starve. Before long they were two emotionally and spiritually famished people weakly attacking each other out of resentment. Chuck was not an emotional nourisher. Melinda was. For years, Melinda had offered Chuck nourishment, but she had received virtually none. Eventually she faded. Then Chuck, resenting her lack of nourishing, blamed her for what was going on, and it became a complex mess.

When a relationship has deteriorated, it is frequently because two starving people are each justifiably crying out for what they both need.

Jim Makes a New Choice and Sets New Boundaries

The night I spent with Terri and Jim at their farmhouse, they began to take a new look at their relationship. Around nine o'clock Terri finally had had enough of the tension and excused herself to go to bed early. That left Jim and me to sit in front of the fire and talk.

"She's been a little edgy lately," Jim said, referring to Terri.

"I noticed," I said straightforwardly. "Care to talk about it?"

"To tell the truth, I would," Jim said as he turned a log in the fireplace, "if you don't mind listening."

"Shoot," I invited.

Jim told a painfully common story. He and his wife had lived in a nearby city, but they had thought that moving into the country would be good for the family, especially the kids. He had a good paying job with the power company, and their city property had sold at a high price so they were able to buy their small farm, remodel the house, and settle in to what seemed to be a pretty nice existence. But living in paradise had not been all that they imagined.

Jim and I talked about all that had occurred in the five years since their move, and one factor stood out larger than the rest.

"You say that your job is still in the city, even though you live here in the mountains?" I asked.

"Yeah," Jim answered. "We decided that I would sacrifice my time to commute to the plant where I work."

"Hasn't that been painful?" I asked.

"More than I realized," Jim replied. "I thought it would be a fatherly thing for me to do, but I've grown to resent the drive. It sometimes takes me more than two hours each way. I generally don't get home until about 8:30 in the evening."

"Jim," I continued, "do you have any idea what the impact of all that has been on your marriage? I don't know what else is going on between you and Terri, but I don't see how you could possibly nourish your relationship when you are gone as much as you describe."

"I guess I thought that she and the kids would be so happy here, that would be all they needed," Jim answered. "Most of the executives at my company work long hours and are away from their families so I thought this was normal.

"You know," he said, "several years ago our marriage was having trouble, and we couldn't quite put our finger on the problem, but at that time I was working long hours and even though we lived near the plant, I was not home very much. Then I fell from a ladder at work and seriously injured myself. It took six weeks of recovery, mostly flat on my back, to get well again, and Terri and I realized at the end of those six weeks that we were friends again! We had drifted far apart and had spent little time together, but neither of us had considered that anything but normal. Now we're in the same boat and, once again, I have not recognized the problem."

In the Bible, Jesus is described as nourishing his bride—the church—and caring for her tenderly, as a gardener cares for a precious plant. This imagery is also used as an example of how a husband should care for his wife. When the gardener notices that the plant is fading and withering, he doesn't beat it with his hoe and give it lectures about how faded it looks. He renews his efforts to care for the plant so it can regain its strength and grow.

The distress in Jim and Terri's marriage was predictable. Even though their experiment with country living had started well, it had been only a matter of time until Terri began feeling lonely. When she tried to communicate that to Jim, he was defensive and took comfort in the fact that he loved his family enough to sacrifice his personal schedule for them. He felt that Terri should honor him for his long hours on the road. So, not only was there little time to nourish his marriage, but he lost any incentive to try because his wife was telling him how unhappy she was, which made him angry.

I kept contact with Jim and Terri and learned that he later made the dramatic decision to leave the power company to become a partner in a business in his small community. He had made an expensive choice, but not nearly as expensive as the previous one. Under his new schedule, he would have more time to nourish those whom he loved.

Yes, you may feel famished yourself and resent the lack of nourishment from your spouse, but an important step is to give nourishment, and to gently encourage your husband or wife to think about giving once again as well. There is an epidemic of withering women married to famished men who are rearing malnourished children in anemic neighborhoods. Even some of the leisure time activity people choose is destructive rather than sustaining.

Perhaps I'm guilty of painting too bleak a picture but I'm describing how many burned-out families actually feel. I'm also describing some of what I've felt myself during periods in my own life when I have been consumed by my schedule and responsibilities, and I've been duped into thinking that being busy was somehow a tribute to my fatherhood. It was when my kids started calling me "Uncle Daddy" that I realized things needed to change!

Ways to Nourish Your Marriage

There are a limitless number of pathways toward nourishment in a marriage, but some emerge as being at the top of the list. I've already emphasized one of the most important in the story of Jim and Terri: time.

Spending time together is supremely nourishing, and anyone who thinks that marriage is going to stay alive without the partners spending significant amounts of time together is probably going to face a day of reckoning. Couples who find themselves in the middle of crisis will sometimes find that devoting time to the marriage will be one of the most important steps toward getting through the crisis.

It is also important that we discover what a spouse considers to be nourishing. Sometimes we find ourselves preparing and dishing out emotional meals that the other person really does not like and is not nourished by. It is worth the effort to try to understand what will fill your hungry or thirsty mate's needs. I talk about this throughout my book *Love, No Strings Attached*, which will give you further insight into the exchanging of love in meaningful ways.

Lack of nourishment in a marriage is one common problem. Another problem, which often causes people to make unwise choices, is their ability to hold unrealistic fantasies about what the marriage relationship should be.

· · · · · · · · ·

Unrealistic Fantasies

When things are painful in life, or in a marriage, it is easy for us to take refuge in our imagination and daydream about the nourishment that we would like. The ability to envision the future or to daydream about nourishing things is a gift from God. The imagination is the tool we use to project, to plan, to conceive of future choices, to anticipate the good, or to prepare for the bad.

There are times when the imagination can help a person survive deprivation. Children who live in abuse frequently retreat into fantasies to get through the day. Prisoners and hostages daydream about what they are going to do when they get out. I remember interviewing Katherine Kolb after she had been held captive by a group of terrorists in the Middle East for almost two years; she spent hours dreaming of McDonald's hamburgers and hot fudge sundaes. When she finally arrived home in the United States, she had her driver stop at McDonald's on the way to her house.

Healthy daydreams and fantasies are not too far from reality, but unhealthy fantasies are quite different. The use of the imagination becomes destructive when the fantasies we are having are so unrealistic and so perfect that the real world could never live up to them. Fantasies are also unhealthy when we are continually and almost obsessively retreating to another world, instead of being able to have an influence on the world in which we are living.

In my experience, this is a frequent problem when we feel helpless and hopeless about our conditions. If, when I was growing up, I learned to escape from reality as a way of coping with pain, it will be easy to continue that habit in adulthood. If I never learned that there are choices available to me and boundaries in my life and the lives of others, if I never learned how to recognize and respond to my needs, then the only thing left is for me to desperately imagine what could have been or what I wish really existed. Under those circumstances we tend to hold on to a fantasy, which is based on unrealistic perfection, and nothing in our real world will ever live up to it. Additionally, if you ever take steps to pursue an unrealistic and perfectionistic fantasy, the bubble will be broken and you'll discover that what you thought was there is not there.

A close friend of mine, whom I will call Barry, once shared with me that he had become obsessed with thinking about a girl who had attended his church when he was a teenager. "I see her smile. I dream about her body. I meditate on her mannerisms. I even think about what it would be like to be married to her. I can't get her out of my mind."

Barry and I talked about this from time to time, and he came to realize that his obsession was due partly to the fact that he had grown up in an alcoholic home. His ability to fantasize had helped him cope. He also realized that things were being made worse for him at this time because of some tension in his marriage. He began to see that he didn't need to feel helpless, and that he could take some steps toward a more nourishing relationship with his wife.

Something interesting happened in the middle of all that, however. "I've learned a lesson," Barry told me one morning at breakfast.

"What's that?" I asked.

"Remember the girl from my youth group in church that I told you about, the one I can't get out of my mind?"

"Yeah," I answered.

"Well, I saw her last month. In fact, I spent a little time with her."

"How'd that happen?" I asked.

"The man who was pastor of the church at the time retired, and there was a dinner in his honor. I was asked to be the master of ceremonies and to serve on the committee planning the dinner and, without my knowing it, she had been asked to serve on the committee too."

"How'd it go?" I asked, almost afraid to hear the answer.

"At first, I was secretly thrilled that she was on the committee. It took only one committee meeting, however, for me to realize that she was not what I had expected."

"In what way?" I asked.

"She was very nice and on the surface was the kind of person I remember, but I was shocked to find she was very different from the kind of person I had imagined. During one of the meetings, for example, there was a discussion during which I realized she has a lot of racial prejudice. There were other indications that she is a very rigid and legalistic person. That didn't appeal to me at all. I never imagined her like that!"

"How do you feel about her now?" I asked.

"I've thought about that," Barry responded. "She still occupies a special place in my heart and probably always will, but I have definitely realized that I have been secretly comparing my wife and my marriage to an illusion."

A Word of Encouragement Remember the principle that your own nourishment is your own responsibility. I appeal to you to first think about the choices you are making for your own nourishment. One of the traps is to blame your spouse, or even the kids, for the fact that you are not a nourished person. There isn't anything or anybody who is standing in the way of your experimenting with some of the things you may have always wanted to do. Your parents or your brothers and sisters may have treated you badly, and may still be doing so, but the power to decide to get help for your hurt is in your hands. If today has been a day without some kind of a "snack" for your heart, no one is to blame but yourself, because even if those who are supposed to offer you nourishment don't do it, you don't need to live a life without nourishment. Get involved with nourishing activities. Enrich your spiritual life. Give of yourself to others. Accomplish a goal that has been sitting on the back burner.

All of this is fairly simple and clear, I'm sure, but it is still overlooked in many marriages. Let me encourage you to think about what you can do to regain some of the feelings you used to enjoy as young lovers. Do you and your spouse need the nourishment of time together? Or the nourishment of encouraging each other? Or the nourishment of helping each other? Or the nourishment of the physical and sexual expression of love? Or the nourishment of rethinking work or volunteer responsibilities in favor of your marriage? Or the nourishment of setting aside specific time in your schedule for your family?

CHAPTER 9

Nourishing
Your
Children

I will never forget reading an article several years ago in one of the Sunday supplement magazines, which featured interviews with several successful men who were now in their seventies or eighties. They were asked to review their lives and comment on their failures and successes. One thing that sticks in my mind was that all of them said that they regretted that they did not spend more time with their families, especially their young children.

I thought, *What a tragedy! To be in the closing season of life and have gained world recognition but to have missed the once-in-a-lifetime opportunity to nourish and be nourished by your children.*

Yet we do it all the time.

A face comes to my mind, that of a nine-year-old girl named Wendy, the daughter of Brian and Carol, a businessman and his wife who attended our church. They had one other child, a son who was about five years old.

Wendy's parents were fine people, and her mother was one of those who was very active in the church.

One of the things I remember most about Wendy was that every time I saw her, she would give me a big hug. At first, I thought it was just because she was affectionate. Over time, however, I came to realize that her hugs were more than just a pastoral greeting. She was starving for a father's attention, and whenever she hugged me or some of the other men in the church, it was a little "snack" of what she needed.

One time I took Carol aside after an event at the church and talked to her about it. "Wendy's a treasure," I told her. "But I've noticed that she is collecting hugs from every man she can find, and I sense a hunger inside her. Doesn't she get affection from her father?"

Carol's eyes filled with tears. "Brian loves the kids, I know that," she told me. "But between the fact that he is gone so much of the time with his business, and that he is the kind of person who just does not express anything from deep inside, I know Wendy is suffering. She is a great little girl, and I'm proud of her, but she's already learned how to be somewhat emotionless, and I'm worried about that."

"Does Brian realize any of this?"

"I don't think he recognizes how bad it is," Carol replied. "We've talked about it, and Brian does feel bad about being away from home a lot, but he argues that he has to do it in order to keep his business alive. I guess he just views it as a necessary evil. Even when he is home, however, he doesn't realize how little emotional contact there is between him and Wendy."

Many months later Brian and Carol were having some trouble in their marriage. One morning after a men's breakfast, Brian asked if he could talk to me about it. We stood in the church's parking lot, leaning against his car, and talked for more than an hour. During the conversation I found an opportunity to talk about Wendy.

"She needs the nourishment of a dad," I suggested. "I know that you love her and are committed to her, but how do you nourish her emotionally?" I asked.

Brian thought for only a brief moment, then said quietly, "I don't know."

"Did you realize, Brian, that Wendy is so apparently hungry for the affection of a father that she sometimes seeks it from some of the other men in the church?" I then told him about the fact that on Sunday I could count on Wendy giving me a kind of hug that, although it did not seem inappropriate, was nonetheless distinctive because of the craving that seemed to go along with it.

One of the reasons Brian and Carol were going through some strife in their marriage was because Carol was trying to get Brian to realize how much their kids needed from him that they were not getting. The observations I shared with him about Wendy jolted him, and that, along with all that Carol had been trying to communicate, finally broke through to Brian.

A couple of weeks later he told me, "I love my kids, and I love Wendy very much, but I didn't realize how little I was personally offering to them and how much they needed from me. I guess I thought Carol was doing that job at home while I was doing the job away from home."

Brian also came to realize that because his own parents had not communicated love in personal ways, he had never learned that either. It was an important season of insight for him, and resulted in a commitment to nourish his children, especially Wendy, in new ways.

. . . .
Kids Need Nourishment

The importance of nourishment in the lives of children cannot be overemphasized. A friend of mine who is an expert on world hunger says that the most pitiful suffering in a famine is among the children. The same is true in the famine of emotional and spiritual nourishment that is occurring in Western culture; the children are the ones who are suffering the most. They are alarmingly malnourished, and they are supposed to be the fathers and the mothers of the next generation.

I am not being completely critical of us moms and dads. I firmly believe that we parents would die for our children. Our culture has lost an understanding, however, of the life-altering importance of providing all forms of nourishment, physical, emotional, and spiritual, to our children, especially during their early years.

In some homes Mom and Dad don't nourish each other, and they are not nourishing the children. These children are being put into childcare settings operated by owners and employees who are not nourished by their jobs, while Mom and Dad work in places that are not nourishing to either of them. That may seem like an exaggeration, but it's more often true than we might realize.

A Mom Who Hadn't Considered the Nourishment Factor

One day on "TableTalk" I had a memorable conversation with a wonderful single mom who was struggling with the decision about moving to a different state. I'll call her Kate.

"How do I know what is the best decision and if God even wants me to move?" she asked.

I talked with Kate for several minutes, and one of the things that kept recurring in her comments was the fact that she was looking for a house that would be cheaper than the one she now owned. She wanted to sell her city home and use the equity to buy something larger in a part of the country where housing was less expensive.

"If God gives you any clear direction where to move," I told Kate, "do it. If that doesn't happen, you are responsible for making the wisest decision you can."

"But that's what I'm having trouble with," she complained. "I don't want to blow it."

"There probably isn't just one 'right' decision," I told her. "There are many choices that probably would be good ones. You'll have to think and pray about all of them. Let me give you one suggestion about decision-making that might be helpful.

"When you look five or ten years down the road, which decision, as best as you can determine, is going to be the most nourishing to you and your daughter, and which one one will allow you to reach any other goals or priorities you have?"

I encouraged Kate to consider whether her choice would be one which would surround her and her daughter with friendship or, if it was important to her, with family. What about a church home and Christian support? What were her daughter's goals?

We talked in those terms for several minutes, then Kate took a deep breath and said, "You know, I haven't thought very much about any of those questions."

As we talked, Kate realized that the overriding reason she wanted to move was because she had come to the conclusion that to live in her city in southern California, which had very expensive housing, didn't make sense from a financial standpoint. She had spent a lot of time with financial advisors and had somehow gotten to the place where her measurement of success in life was having more property for less money.

"It makes a lot of sense to get as much for your money as possible," I told her, "but that shouldn't be the only reason for making a change. If your city has all the other ingredients that you and your daughter want and need, and if you can afford to live there, you might be living in the right place."

Kate sounded a little astonished. "To tell you the truth, I

do like it here," she said. "My friends are here, the church that has helped change our lives is here. In fact, my daughter really doesn't want to move!"

I said, "Kate, from the standpoint of personal nourishment, it sounds as if neither you nor your daughter would really choose to leave town."

"I guess I just allowed myself to be overtaken by my feeling that it's stupid to live in a house that is worth so much money compared with houses in other cities. I figured we'd find new friends, a new school, and a new church. That would be fine if I had any other good reason to move, but I don't, and my daughter and I have been fussing over that for weeks."

"The decision is up to you," I cautioned. "Think about it for a few days or weeks from the standpoint of nourishment before you make a final decision."

I want to encourage parents: Make decisions that take the nourishment of your children into account. You will never be sorry for launching a child who has experienced as much healthy nourishment as possible into the world.

Unfortunately some parents' natural nourishment of their children has been twisted by two common parenting myths.

Fear of Spoiling the Child

I remember a call from a young mother who was struggling with how to respond to her one-year-old son. She was under a lot of pressure from one of the leaders in her church who had taught a class on parenting. He advocated ignoring the sleeping and eating needs of infants. He felt that if you allow the child to dictate when to eat or when to sleep, you would be teaching the child that he is the center of the universe, and that would be unhealthy. Another version of this mind-set is the old "You must feed an infant on a strict schedule" injunction.

I agree that, as children grow older, they need to recognize their needs are not the only ones in the household. Neither should they think that the world is not going to stop when they demand it. I think it is going too far, however, to assign such conscious strategies to babies who obviously need to be fed or changed or held or rocked to sleep. To be sure, it can be argued that there is a danger that the child could develop the habit of manipulating parents and the home environment, but that is not a reason to pretend as though there is no hunger or other need, and it is not a reason to get into the habit of ignoring hunger or need.

This young mother was being told not to respond to her baby, except at certain specified times, and even then to regulate what she did. I suggested to her, "Let's talk about physical nourishment for a minute. As your child grows, he is going to get hungry regularly. A normal child is going to consume food in a way that satisfies his appetite and his need for nourishment. Can you imagine how the child would be affected if you only allowed him to eat at certain times and in amounts that you regulated without regard to his need? Don't you think that a boy who spends his entire childhood being hungry, and never quite experiencing true nourishment, will be more likely to be preoccupied with food and more likely to "cling" to whatever potential sources of nourishment are available, like drugs or sex. On the other hand, the satisfied child would have the confidence that when the time comes for food, he's going to get what he needs."

I can say this: My wife and I have reared seven children through infancy and early childhood on the principle of responding to their natural needs. Believe me, we're not sorry for it.

Another fear is a kissing cousin to the first. It's the fear that the child won't grow to be independent of the parent.

The Fear That the Child Won't Grow to Be Independent

I recently had a friend tell me, "I don't do as much with my son or for him as I want to, because I am afraid he will have a hard time detaching from me and living an adult life."

I think that is backwards. A nourished child is the one who is ready to get up from the table and walk into other areas of life. A child who has learned how to make nourishing choices is the one who will live that way as an adult. Don't ever resist giving a child the hugs or the gift of time that says, "I love you, I value you, I'm really proud of you." And that doesn't come just through isolated communications. It comes from being nourished by massive amounts of one another's presence, or keeping the "cup" reasonably filled. When the cup gets empty, it takes more than a planned moment of "quality" time to start filling it again.

On the heels of that I would advise you to remember that the number one need in your child's life is to be nourished by you. Not anyone else, but you. No one is more important to a child than Mom or Dad or whoever is occupying that important position in the child's life.

Time Is Nourishment

As with marriage, the number one way to nourish children is to spend *time* with them. There is no substitute, no effective nourishing, for spending time with our children.

Our culture has created a myth of "quality time." I bought into that lie myself for a while. I would try to plan "quality" time with my family. It soon became obvious to me, however, that "quality" time was actually an excuse for not spending a "quantity" of time with them.

If there is any crisis that is facing our homes, it is the crisis of not spending time together. It is fascinating to me that we are wringing our hands, wondering why kids are not doing well in school and why they are immersing themselves in drugs and alcohol and sex when some of what is happening to children is so clear.

It's not hard to understand how a starving person will say "yes" to drugs, alcohol, sex, and other alarming behaviors. Teenagers are not experimenting with drugs and sex because they think it is good or right. (That's why they keep it a secret.) They are involved in those activities partly because of the sheer enormity of their hunger and the willingness on the part of people around them to take advantage of their vulnerability. Anyone is tempted to compromise a lot of standards in his life if he's starving. Mom and Dad and kids need to be able to spend more *time* together.

I received a call on the radio just this week from a man who was upset by the actions of his twelve-year-old daughter.

"She came home with a bleached streak in her hair," he told me, "and I got mad and took away her makeup, her hair dryer, and all the other stuff she uses to try to look like her friends."

"What did that bleached streak mean to you?" I asked him.

"I don't know," he answered. "It just seemed to me that she was starting to look like the kind of kids I don't like."

"Are those the kids she hangs around with?"

"Yeah, I guess they are," he admitted.

"Why do you think she hangs around with them?" I asked.

"I don't know, and that's what frustrates me," he answered with emotion. "She's a Christian girl and doesn't have any business with friends like that."

"Your daughter, like any twelve-year-old, has deep needs for nourishment," I said. "She is obviously getting a lot of nourishment from this group of friends, so much so that she wants to identify with them."

"What can I do about all that?" the caller asked. "This group of kids is no good."

"Think about it for a moment," I suggested. "How are you responding to your daughter's need for nourishment?"

"My wife and I do the best we can, but I have to drive a long way to work, and she works too. We're just kind of busy," the man confessed.

"I know that feeling," I replied, "but something is going to have to change, and you and your wife are going to have to ask the Lord to help you be sensitive to more of your daughter's needs for nourishment, especially those needs that can only come from Mom and Dad.

"I admit that not all of your daughter's needs must be met in your home. As she grows, friends and teachers and other adults will meet some of her needs. She should know what is going on outside of her home and learn to make her own nourishing choices. But right now I think she might be starving for the kind of nourishment that needs to begin at home. Storming into her room and taking all her beauty supplies away from her will only make the problem worse."

Kids of all ages need to be touched by their folks, they need to be able to watch their family and learn from them, they need to have you there so important, spontaneous discussions can take place. They need their folks to be aware of what's going on in their lives so they can offer encouragement and validation, as well as correction.

This is one of the reasons why my wife and I have elected to home school our children. I feel a responsibility before God to invest myself in the lives of my children, and that is impossible to do under the typical American schedule. I'll never forget when one of my daughters was in eighth grade and attending a quality school. She was up at 6:30 A.M., had to get to school by 7:30 A.M., spent the entire day with her peers and teachers, had extra activities in the afternoon, a brief time to spend doing whatever she wanted with her friends in the late afternoon, then had enough homework to keep her up until late each night. I loved her. She loved me. But it was literally impossible for me to compete with these overwhelming influences. Less than twenty percent of her nourishment was coming from our home and only about one or two percent was coming from me.

Is it any wonder that kids are living their own lives in rebellion to their homes and families? Do we really believe that other people and activities can replace parental nourishment? I have watched in frustration (and so have many professional teachers) as our society continues to advocate or require parents to make choices that are destructive to the home, and then society expects schools and teachers to make things right.

Any professional teacher will tell you that the place of prime importance is the home. Teachers don't want to have to carry the emotional burdens of malnourished kids. Some of them courageously try but, in general, the school cannot replace the loss of self-esteem, values, and other traditionally homespun qualities that are missing from the lives of our kids.

Next time you are making a major decision about career or home or family, ask yourself, "What will be the most nourishing to everyone involved—to me, to my family, to my community?"

I recently talked with a woman on the radio who, after a lengthy conversation, admitted that she was about to accept a job that was not nourishing to her at the expense of caring for her child, which was nourishing to her, because of the urging of her husband. On top of all of that, her child was going to be cared for by a relative who didn't want the responsibility. Why was she considering this option? "Because it seemed right."

Right by what standard? Certainly not by the standard of nourishment. This mom realized that she was going to be more nourished by staying at home. Her child was going to be more nourished. Her husband would be more nourished, whether he realized it or not, because he would have a nourished child and nourishing wife. And the relative who was going to care for the child would also be more nourished for not having to accept that unwanted responsibility!

Let me say that I do understand there are many parents who need to choose preschool or childcare because of having to work or because of being a single parent. My comments are not meant to condemn those who find themselves in those situations. In fact, many don't want to have to make that choice! I do want to be a voice, however, that encourages parents to take a fresh look at the long-term value of choosing what is most nourishing for their children, when possible. I believe nothing is a good substitute for children to be nourished by their own folks.

As a child grows, the needs will change and the type of nourishment we offer will need to be reviewed. Once again, a pertinent question for each of us as parents is, "How am I nourishing my child? What actual investments of sustenance am I making?" As I have asked that of parents, the answer is frequently, "I work hard and supply well for my family." God bless you for that. Only a father and mother who have sacrificed for their children know how fulfilling that is. But folks, that doesn't completely nourish our children. In fact, many of us have worked hard to provide for our families in a way that has actually left our children malnourished in their relationship with us. I have become convinced that for most Americans, especially in certain communities, the biggest enemy to the family is the pace of our lives. We can become seduced into thinking that we are so busy and accomplishing so much that it must be of benefit to us and our family.

Unfortunately our society does not value children as much as we did in the past, so it is easy to make decisions at their expense. If you are a young woman, for example, who is sacrificing your energy and your time and your health to get through medical school, you are valued and honored by those around you. If you're going through the same sacrifice, however, to have your fourth child, your good judgment is questioned.

In the secret places of our culture we do terrible things to children. We abuse them, resent them, and even abort them. We consider them accessories—or resented tag-alongs—to whatever we've defined life to be. With that view, why would I ever adjust my career goals or spending habits in order to accommodate my children?

Some children of our culture are as famished emotionally and spiritually as kids in Ethiopia are starving physically. I see some of the same looks of sadness and hunger on the faces of American kids, looking through the wire fences of some of our institutions, as I see on the faces of children in the Third World countries as they look through the wire fences of refugee camps.

A guest on my program once encouraged me to think about the kids in places like Africa, who are lonely, home-less, and hungry. He described the conditions in such effective terms that I, along with a lot of those who were listening, was ready to make a phone call or copy down an address that would allow me to actually sponsor one of those children. My listeners and I wanted to make life better for all of them.

The guest paused, and during that moment of silence, I was sitting on the edge of my chair, waiting for his next instruction as to what I could do to help the kids. He finally said, "Now, take that intensity and that compassion and that desire to make a difference in a child's life and go home and give it to your children."

He was right. It is sometimes easier to see the need in a child thousands of miles away than it is to sense what is needed at home.

Our children not only need heaping amounts of healthy

nourishment from us, but we are also teaching them how to nourish the generation that follows them. It's an investment that has far-reaching implications.

Let's endeavor to launch our children into life with a basic foundation of nourishment that will serve them, and others, for a long time to come.

And that includes spiritual nourishment, which we'll look at in Part Four, an essential part of being a nourished person.

PART 4

Spiritual
Nourishment

CHAPTER 10

....

The First Step
Toward
Spiritual Nourishment

I will never forget Jack, a man who had the reputation for not having any need for God. His wife, Helen, attended a church where I was on staff. Jack and Helen were the kind of people who seemed to have what most people wanted. They were comfortable financially. Some considered them rich. They lived in a large, beautiful home on the side of a hill with a view that, on a clear day, stretched from the middle of the Los Angeles basin all the way to the ocean. Jack was a semi-retired businessman and an avid outdoorsman. Helen was a successful interior designer. They had raised two daughters who seemed to be pursuing life in a way that pleased both of their parents.

One of the major struggles in Helen's life, however, was Jack's lack of interest in God. He didn't object to Helen's involvement; in fact, he would cheerfully attend some of the seasonal or special functions at the church. He didn't seem opposed to anything we believed or stood for; he just didn't seem interested. Helen had been in my office more than once with tears in her eyes, expressing her concern about Jack spiritually and asking for prayer.

I really liked Jack and got to know him as best I could. He and I could sit and talk about fishing, for example, for hours. He also had an interest in aviation, and that gave us another topic to kick around from time to time. There would even be times when I felt that he would zip open his heart and talk openly about deeper issues.

I remember, for example, one afternoon when I was riding with him in his car to a church event that his wife had helped organize, and I asked about some of his background. He told me a long story about his deep desire as a youth to become a military pilot, and how, after graduating from college and enlisting in the Navy, he was devastated to be assigned to navigation school instead of flight school. After the Navy, which included service in World War II, he experimented with various jobs and careers and eventually settled into being a contractor.

In other words, Jack showed no opposition to his wife's faith and circulated comfortably among her Christian friends and, when the opportunity arose, would talk straightforwardly, albeit unemotionally, about his life. In it all, however, much to the frustration of Helen and others, there didn't seem to be the slightest spiritual hunger. Faith seemed irrelevant to him in every way.

One afternoon when I was helping prepare for a conference at our church, I was given an urgent message to call Helen. "Jack's father passed away day before yesterday," she told me. "There isn't going to be a funeral, but the family would like to have a short graveside service and Jack wants to know if you would do it."

"Of course," I replied. "Tell Jack I'll be over this evening to talk about it."

Later as I was driving to Jack and Helen's house I thought to myself, *Isn't it interesting that this apparently irreligious man has asked for a religious service for his father.*

Jack and Helen and I spent almost two hours together. We briefly discussed what he wanted for the graveside service and talked a lot about his father, whom I had never met, then ate a light supper that Helen had prepared. Later, other members of the family arrived, and after introducing myself to them, I decided to leave and let them be alone.

As I walked toward my car, I noticed a lighted cigarette in the darkness and saw that it was Jack, sitting on the edge of a large stone fountain near the side of his house. "Excuse me, Jack," I apologized. "I didn't realize you were out here. I'm going to head back home but if I can do anything for you, please call."

It took Jack a few moments to reply, and when he did I realized he was crying. "You've already been a big help, Rich," he said. "Thanks for coming tonight and for being available for the service."

"You're a friend, Jack," I replied. "Thank you for calling me."

"Have you got another minute for me to ask you a question?" he asked.

"Yes," I responded and sat on the edge of the fountain next to him.

"Tell me about heaven," Jack said. "Do you really believe in heaven, and if you do, do you think my dad is there?"

I tried not to show my surprise at hearing that kind of question from Jack, the stalwart businessman who never admitted that he had any needs and certainly no need for God.

"Yes, I believe in heaven," I replied. "I can't speak for God on behalf of your father, but I believe God will make a just decision about him."

"You mean nobody knows whether they are going to heaven?" Jack asked.

"I didn't say that," I replied. "I believe there is a clear decision that each of us needs to make about Jesus Christ that brings us into a relationship with God and gives us confidence about eternity. I simply do not know what kind of decision your father made about Christ. I never met him or talked with him about it and, according to what you have told me tonight, your father never said much to you about his faith. Even so, Jack, you or I or anyone else could not speak for your father and whatever choices he made about God. That's something only he and God would know."

There was a long silence. "Jack," I asked softly, "how are you and God getting along?"

Jack sat in silence for a few moments. Then, crushing his cigarette in an ash tray he had brought from the house, he took a deep breath and said, "You know what? I pray a lot. I've never told anybody that before, but I really do pray. When I'm hunting or fishing or just in the out-of-doors, I have a lot of thoughts about God and I talk to him. Lately, I've been talking to him about my dad because I knew he was sick and was going to die."

"How long has this been going on?" I asked.

Jack took a deep breath and said, "I don't know. All my life I guess. I've just never been the kind of person to talk about it."

Jack went on to share with me an emotional story from when he was in World War II and when a buddy of his, a committed Christian, was killed. Jack had always felt guilty that his friend had been killed instead of him and, along with it, he had a haunting conviction that God must have wanted him to live for some reason. "I guess I've always been trying to figure out what God's purpose is in allowing me to live," Jack admitted. "I especially think about it at a time like this, when someone has died."

Jack and I had a fascinating discussion that evening, which revealed that much of his success in business had secretly been a part of his campaign to thank God for letting him live and to try to discover what God's purpose was in his life. He had never disclosed that to anyone because, in a childlike way, it was intimidating to him to talk about anything from his heart, especially about God. Even his wife knew nothing of his spiritual thoughts.

The most startling point of the conversation was when Jack confessed that he had asked Christ into his life as he was driving down the freeway one day while listening to a Christian radio program! All this from a man who had the reputation of not needing God in his life! He had been hungry after all. He was just the kind of person who never let his hunger show.

The postscript was that Jack asked me not to share any of this with his wife, and I never did. It was long after that he finally was willing to entrust her with some knowledge of his spiritual life and decisions. I have often thought how interesting it was that in a world where a person's secret life often includes crime or pornography, here was a man who had a secret life with God.

. . . .

Our Ever-present Spiritual Hungers

Spiritual hungers are no less natural than physical or emotional hungers, no less designed by God and no less important to recognize and to nurture. In fact, in my view, they are more important because they address the deepest part of us, and they are of eternal significance. These hungers include the need to know God, to be loved by him, to love him, to be touched by his power, to know what his purpose is for our lives. We may try to ignore or combat these spiritual hungers or hide them, but they are always there.

We are essentially spiritual creatures. The evidence of

that is overwhelming. Every culture in the world and every known culture in history has shown evidence of people reaching out from their spiritual hunger. Research and surveys indicate that even in countries where organized religion has become stale and ineffective, the people believe in God, and the majority of them pray, especially in crisis.

The dramatic events in Eastern Europe have spotlighted how decades of atheism and communism did not eliminate individual spiritual hunger. The communists may have outlawed religion and emptied or regulated the churches, but in both Eastern Europe and in China people who were rendered poor in money and possessions and even personal freedom became rich in spiritual nourishment. The true church, meaning individuals who have come to know Christ, actually grew despite the persecution.

When I was in grade school, I somehow developed the impression that the entire world was filled with atheists, and that there was this tiny, trembling group of Christians whose job it was to evangelize all those atheists. I thought that we should "go into the world and argue evolution with every creature." As I grew older, I began to realize that there are not very many true atheists at all. Over the years of my ministry both as a pastor and on the radio I have not run across very many true atheists. I've talked with a lot of honest-hearted agnostics who admit that they're searching and interested in knowing the truth and can't say they've found it yet, but very few atheists. That's because atheism is unnatural.

Most atheists, in my view, are people who have had various kinds of personal or religious experiences that have turned them off to faith. They have either closed themselves off from spiritual hunger or are pretending not to have it. For them, religion is painful. Or they feel so completely ineligible spiritually, because of childhood destruction, such as physical, emotional or sexual abuse, they just close themselves off from the subject. I once interviewed a man on my program who had researched the lives of three or four of the leading atheists of the twentieth century and found that each of them had experienced childhood abuse, and this, he felt, had played a major role in their rejection of God.

Many other atheists are victims of what I call "spiritual abuse." In other words, that which was supposed to have nourished the individual has been twisted by other people and used to hurt. It's very similar to the experience of a person who has been sexually molested and who, as a result, is cut off from enjoying healthy sex and, in fact, may be unable to enter into any healthy relationships.

The point is that spiritual hunger is one of the drives in the human heart that explains a lot about individuals and societies. To ignore that hunger or to fail to recognize it is not normal.

· · · · · · · · ·
What Are We Hungry For?

One of the perplexities about spiritual hunger is that there are so many different ideas about what is supposed to be spiritually nourishing. The old adage, "Don't talk about religion and politics," was originated by somebody who undoubtedly experienced the jeopardy of trying. Everybody's got his own opinion.

It is also discouraging to the spiritual seeker to look at the history of religion and see the wars that have happened between people of differing religious beliefs and the inhumanity of certain religious leaders or movements.

I remember a discussion I had about that with a cab driver in Richmond, Virginia. We were making our way through morning traffic to the airport, and he was a chatty kind of guy, talking about anything that came to mind. He asked me what I was doing in Richmond. "I was here to speak at a church," I replied.

"Oh," he remarked. "Are you a pastor?"

It's always interesting to me how some people will immediately change their demeanor when they learn I'm a minister. When I told him "yes," he suddenly sat a little more upright, grabbed the steering wheel with both hands, and, glancing back and forth between the road and the rearview mirror, he said, "Gee, I'm sorry, Reverend. My language has been a little saucy. I hope I didn't offend you."

I chuckled and said, "Thank you for thinking of me, but I'd like you to just be yourself. And you don't have to call me 'Reverend.' My name is Rich."

That seemed to put him at ease. He then launched into a detailed defense about why he didn't go to church anymore. One of his complaints, he said, was that religion had caused so much heartache for so many people throughout the centuries.

"You're right there," I agreed. "Some of the worst instances of people being cruel and unfair to other people have been in the name of the church."

"So how can you be a minister?" he asked bluntly. "How can you stand being associated with stuff like that? I don't want to go near it."

"Because I don't think the problem has been uniquely a religious one," I replied. "It's a people problem. Wherever there are people, there are people problems. There is the danger of a leader or a group doing a lot of stupid things to other people. If it only happened in connection with religion, we could consider religion to be the difficulty, but some of the most hideous treatment of people in modern history has not been associated with theology or the church. Hundreds of thousands of people have been tortured or killed in the name of communism, for example, which is officially atheistic."

"Yeah, I guess you're right there," he agreed.

"A lot of attention is given to the organizations or individuals who have been destructive," I continued, "but that does not mean they represent all believers anymore than a cab driver who is a rapist and a thief represents all cab drivers."

With his defenses lowered, the cab driver and I had a good conversation about personal faith. It was clear that he, like all of us, was spiritually hungry and was looking for that which would satisfy his need.

· · · · · · · · · ·

Spiritual Nourishment

There are a lot of beliefs about what is spiritually nourishing, and you'll get a lot of opinions from a lot of people.

I'll give you mine.

If God has created us and if he has created us with a natural hunger for spiritual nourishment, we can determine if we are receiving that nourishment in ways that are similar to the ways we test our physical nourishment, which I mentioned in Chapter 3.

Recognizing Spiritual Nourishment

First, we can be taught by those who have hopefully already learned what is nutritious and what is poisonous. Even if our family did not give us reliable information, we learn as we grow older which sources are most valuable and can be trusted.

Second, we measure nourishment by whether it has truly satisfied our hunger over the long term. The caution, however, is that when we are severely hungry or thirsty, we run the risk of sometimes thinking that almost anything new we've discovered along the way fulfills our need.

Think of a person who has never tasted water, and yet is on a quest to satisfy his thirst because of his need. If the first liquid he finds is gasoline, he may be so overjoyed at having something to drink for the first time in his life that he would think the gasoline is water. He might even go to his friends and say, "I have found it. Come drink with me."

Over time, however, he would find that the gasoline has unwelcome effects on him, and he would ultimately have to admit that it did not satisfy his thirst. In fact, it didn't even taste good. Later he might find something with better flavor, but which still is not nourishing, and would have the same joyful feeling of having "found it." His use of this new liquid might last longer than his use of the gasoline because it tasted better, and it might even address some of his thirst. Yet one of two things would have to happen. He would either have to be honest with himself and admit that he has still not found "it." Or he would discover a fresh, wonderful spring of cool mountain water, and something inside of him would say, "This is truly it!"

For a while, he might be cautious, saying to himself, "I've gone through this before." But the test of time would prove to him that this is, indeed, water, and that would become the standard for him. He might also reflect on the fact that friends and family members had been telling him about this spring and the water there for a long time, but for various reasons he had not responded to what they had to say.

· · · · · · · · · ·

The Answer

I have come to believe that I have been created by God, that I have a natural hunger for spiritual nourishment, and that God has given me ample information for how that hunger can be satisfied. When I partake of it, I'm going to know that it meets my need. I don't have to pretend. I don't have to rationalize. I don't have to force myself to drink gasoline or to eat dirt.

If you were able to sit down with God some cool evening and ask him, "What is going to be the answer to my spiritual hunger," he would point you in the direction of Jesus Christ.

How do I know that?

Two reasons. One is that I am among those who have wandered down the pathway of spiritual hunger, with a few sidetrips along the way, and I have actually experienced what Jesus has to offer. Like the man who finally discovered the spring of water and who never again wondered what would satisfy his thirst, I have partaken of Jesus Christ in a way that has satisfied something so deeply and so fully that I have not thirsted in quite that way again.

Let me make myself clear. I am not saying that I do not have needs. I am not saying that all my questions are answered. I am not saying that I do not struggle with skepticism or doubt.

I am saying that the part of me that used to look longingly at various faiths or various philosophies has had a drink that was like none of the others. That drink was the spiritual counterpart to discovering a wonderful mountain spring! For nearly twenty years, this has nourished my hunger to know who God is.

Second, I believe that regardless of my personal experience, there is testimony from God himself and from the thousands of years of people who have known him that Jesus Christ is the doorway to spiritual nourishment.

God reveals or explains himself to us in a lot of ways, but I have developed a trust in the Bible as being, among other things, a handbook of nourishment for hungry and thirsty people. Actually, the Bible is not just one book, it is a collection of books. Some of them are historic, some are poetic, some are actually prophetic (that's an interesting topic in itself). Through the test of time, however, the Bible has become accepted as a written record of some of the things that God wants us to know and as a reliable measuring stick for discovering what is truly nourishing.

The Benefit of a Measuring Stick

I sometimes go fishing along the California coast where certain kinds of fish cannot be kept legally unless they are a certain length or longer. Some of them must be more than twelve inches. Others must be more than twenty-two inches. One day a friend of mine and I eagerly rushed to the marina, launched his outboard boat, stopped at the bait barge for some anchovies, and embarked upon a day fishing in the Pacific. The only problem was that we forgot to bring anything to measure the fish we caught. All day long we struggled with deciding which fish we could keep and which we would throw back. It was sometimes a matter of opinion. He'd say, "What do you think, Rich. Is that fish over twenty-two inches?"

I'd say, "Yeah, that's a keeper for sure."

Then he'd say, "I don't know. It looks a little short to me."

We returned to shore and actually measured the fish, especially the larger ones; several were longer or shorter than we had thought.

From that time on I started keeping a stick with my fishing gear, which was exactly the size of the minimum length for some of the larger fish and also had some of the other lengths marked along the side. That measuring stick helped me decide what to keep and what to throw back.

That's why God gave us a written record, so we would have a measuring stick to help us decide what to keep and what to throw away. It is a manual for spiritually hungry people, and since it was given to us by the God who made us, it makes sense to trust it.

It's as if a person who had never tasted water had stumbled across a book which contained the history of people who had found water, and that book had stood the test of time. If all of the people who had finally arrived at the spring said, "Yep, the book is right," that would be a sensational discovery.

The problem occurs, of course, when some of the people who have only gotten as far as the gasoline write their own books and testify, "Gas satisfies our thirst." Yet they'll have to do a whole lot of pretending to believe that gas really tastes good. Eventually, if they're really responding to their thirst, they will once again look for water.

In the coming pages, we are going to discuss various ways to experience spiritual nourishment and to nourish others spiritually, but it is critical to start the discussion in the way that we have. It is no accident that the Bible presents Jesus Christ as the "bread of life" and the "drink of living water from which you will never thirst."

The Living Water That Quenches Our Thirst

Each of us is able to drink of the living water that will quench our thirst. Yet we have been cut off from God, because of the disease of sin and because of our tendency to either rebel against authority or to roam down our own pathways. The Bible refers to it as spiritual death. The physical part of us is alive, but another part of us needs to be brought back to life. It is impossible for any of us to bring ourselves back to life on our own. In order to have a relationship with God, our sin needs to be dealt with, because the consequence of sin is to remain spiritually dead forever.

Some people think that Christianity is a religion of guilt trips and judgmentalism. That's because some people and churches have made it that way, but condemnation, like cruelty, comes from other sources, not Christian doctrine. The message about Christ is in contrast with that. Jesus taught that because of God the Father's love for us, his creation, he had a hunger of his own. That hunger was to provide a way for our sin to be dealt with and to once again have relationship with us on a personal level.

God's representatives were not instructed to condemn people to death. They were not running through the streets, pointing their fingers and saying, "I condemn you." Jesus, and those whom he chose to work with him, were not an execution squad that rounded up people in the middle of the city and shot them. They were a rescue squad that went through the cities with passion in their voices and sometimes tears in their eyes saying, "Please listen to us. You are already condemned because of your sin but we have good news: you can be revived. You can have life. You can partake of the single most important nourishment of all—Jesus himself."

In the arrangement that the Father made, Jesus suffered and died as payment for our sin. That is why he is honored as the Savior. He literally died to save us. The message of Christ is that God offers every person the opportunity to be rescued from spiritual death.

How do we receive it? First, by coming to realize the importance of what Christ has done, and the fact that God offers it to us, and the fact that we need it.

Second, by soberly and genuinely recognizing that the pathways we've traveled may have been sincere and even seemed nourishing at moments, but it's time to take God's pathway and to commit our lives to it. If that is our understanding, then there simply needs to be a moment when we tell God that and pledge ourselves to it. In essence, what I'm describing is how to become a Christian. This is the first and most important step in receiving true spiritual nourishment.

The Bible does not require us to join any particular organization or to go through any particular ritual or to adopt any particular appearance. Becoming a Christian is a moment along the pathway of life, wherever we happen to be at the time, when we are finally struck with God's love and what he has done for us and his invitation to commit our lives to him. We decide, in our own way, to say, "Yes!" to him.

It's very much like falling in love and promising your life to another person in marriage. After you meet that person and learn of that person's love and evaluate what it means to commit yourself to that person, and think about it and struggle over it and delight in it, there is finally a day when you wake up and say, "Yes!" You've spent enough time thinking about that "yes" that you know you really mean "yes" and it's "yes" for life. In one way it is uncomplicated and simple. In another way it is the most important decision we will ever make because our spiritual and eternal lives depend on it.

CHAPTER 11

. . . .

Living
a Spiritually
Nourished Life

I was delighted at the prospect of seeing Jim, one of my favorite people from college days. He went to graduate school and then on to a career in New England. I went into radio broadcasting and, at the time, was working for a large "all news" station in Los Angeles. Unfortunately we hadn't had much contact since graduation.

I was also going through the spiritual "blahs." My faith was intact, and I was even involved in some activities that were of help to other people spiritually, but I was dragging, and I didn't fully realize it. Often when things are changing in our lives we don't realize what's going on! Other people can see these changes better than we can.

Jim and I spent a couple of evenings talking about old times and getting caught up to date. We talked honestly about some of the ups and downs of life that we had experienced—and we talked about the Lord.

One of the most significant moments in our time together came when he said, "Rich, you seem to be really dragging right now. Where are you getting support? How are you being nourished spiritually?"

At first, I was a little taken aback by his question. I was used to thinking of myself as the kind of person who was always available to nourish someone else. For a few seconds I was confused and I wanted to say to him, "How dare you view me as needing anything. I'm involved in my church! I'm a person who helps others! I give money to worthy projects! I love the Lord!"

The more I thought about it, however, the more I recognized that his question was right on target. I couldn't think of a single channel of spiritual nourishment that I was taking advantage of, and I had been blinded to it. I had just taken a new job, moved to a new community, and established a relationship with a relatively new church—but without true spiritual nourishment. It was like trying to drive cross-country on one tank of gas. In fact, the conversation with him that evening was probably the most spiritual nourishment I had experienced in months!

· · · · · · · · ·

Steps to Spiritual Nourishment

What, then, are some of the specific choices that we can make to live a spiritually nourished life?

Once again, I rely on the Bible for the best answers to that question.

Jesus gave up some of what it meant to be God in order to live as a man and modeled some of the ways for us to live. As followers of Christ, we actually have the privilege of becoming more like him. Paying attention, then, to some of the ways that Jesus himself received nourishment makes sense.

Anyone who wants to be like Jesus but ignores personal nourishment is missing the point. Jesus ate food, took time away for rest and recreation, slept, traveled to nourishing areas of his world, and devoted himself to various disciplines that are to be a part of our lives as well.

For most of us the word *discipline* means things like jogging a mile a day or avoiding banana cream pie. Those are not bad choices, but that is not the heart of a spiritual discipline. In the Bible, disciplines are actually steps toward nourishment. God is not saying, "I need proof that you love me, so for the next six months I want you to do something loathsome." He is giving us tips from himself, the designer, on what will best nourish us, his creation.

The Nourishment of Solitude

One day as I was preparing to go on the air with my radio program, I paused to quickly look through some of the mail that had accumulated for me. I saw the return address of a cherished friend of mine on one of the letters, so I grabbed that one and took it into the studio with me. Later, during a commercial break, I opened it and read it.

The purpose of the letter, it turned out, was to let me know how excited he was about a new book he had read, and he let me know in the strongest terms that he thought I should read it too. The title of the book was *The Spirit of the Disciplines* by Dr. Dallas Willard. He is the former head of the Philosophy Department at the University of Southern California and currently a professor of philosophy at USC. He is also a committed follower of Jesus Christ and a respected leader and teacher.

I got the book and was deeply affected by it. I felt it was one of the best discussions I had ever read of what is missing from the lives of committed Christians. It took only a second for me to decide I wanted to have him as a guest on my program. We scheduled his visit for a few weeks later.

I began the interview with Dr. Willard by talking about the discipline of solitude.

"If we look at the written record of the life of Jesus," Dr.

Willard said, "we will see that one of the most frequent and important disciplines for him was that of solitude. Jesus spent time alone and on a regular basis."

"That's an alien concept to most of us living in the fast lane," I replied. "I think I like solitude, but whenever I go there I take a multi-function cassette player/CD/radio/TV with me so I won't be so alone!"

"Solitude, and the companion nourishment of silence, are vital," Dr. Willard continued, "because not only do we quiet our own hearts and lives, but we improve the conditions for sensing what God is saying or doing."

"It's always been fascinating to me," I commented, "that on the night before Jesus chose his disciples, he stayed up, spending time in solitude and prayer. I would have imagined that he had a FAX machine to communicate with his father and wouldn't have to pray about the choices at all."

"He wrestled with the rightness of decisions like we do," Dr. Willard responded, "and in solitude and silence he discerned and determined the Father's will."

I haven't always understood the importance of solitude and cannot even say that I knew what to call it, but during a very critical season of my life when I was a young father and trying to determine what God was doing in my life, I discovered solitude without realizing it. For the first time in my life, for example, I started taking nightly walks, usually late at night, and I would spend long periods either pouring out my heart before God or just being silent under the stars. That was also a season that produced the most important spiritual nourishment of my life up to that time. I became excited about spiritual things, almost intoxicated with them at times, and formed a foundation of spiritual understanding that is important to me to this day.

I would also occasionally drive to the seashore and spend time with God there. During times of pain or depression I would go out of town and spend time alone at a motel, or I would travel to a place in a nearby state that is very special to me.

Later, when I was on the staff of a church in central California, I spent hours with God in an almond orchard. The almond trees in that orchard just behind our house heard a lot of my innermost thoughts and dreams, as well as my sins and struggles. I have often thought that it is a good thing they can't talk! Many times, however, I would just walk around the orchard or find a place to sit and enjoy solitude with God.

Sometimes that solitude was filled with joy and praise. Sometimes with tears and pain. Sometimes I'd even walk out to the orchard and not find any solace at all, but over time that exercise of spending time in solitude and silence was powerfully nourishing. I did not do it as an obligation. It was driven by my own hunger and kept alive by the nourishment it offered.

Seeking solitude does not mean having to fly to the mountains or drive to the desert even though those can be nourishing settings. You can find time alone with yourself and with God in the midst of the busiest city. Sometimes it might be for a few minutes, sometimes hours or days. It will include prayer, but should also include being silent and listening. That doesn't mean that you'll hear a voice like an inner radio broadcast, but you'll be in a position to better receive from God, no matter how he chooses to move in your heart and in your understanding.

The Nourishment of Prayer

I received a call recently from a woman who listens to my program in Dallas, Texas. "My son is in his first year of college," she began. "He's having a terrible time. He says his classes are just too hard, and he doesn't think he's going to make it through the first semester."

"How can I help you?" I asked.

"I want to know how to pray for him," she said with a sense of pleading in her voice. "What should I say to God?"

That question suggests that people feel there is a particular procedure for praying, and that if we don't use the right method, it won't work. If I say the wrong words or say them in the wrong way, I will jinx my prayer, and God will not answer it.

A similar call came from a woman who identified herself as Wina. "I'm very excited about a job opportunity that has opened for me," she began. "But I don't know how to pray about it. I'm not sure what to say."

"Prayer is talking honestly with God," I replied. "You should feel the freedom to say to him exactly what is on your heart."

"But I don't know whether it is his will for me to have the job."

"That doesn't mean that you cannot or should not tell him your feelings," I encouraged. "If you're uncertain about whether or not to take the job, tell him. If you're excited and feel that you really want the job, tell him. If you feel that this is the greatest opportunity you've ever had presented to you in your life, tell him. If you feel that it's the most frightening thing you've ever faced, tell him. Spend time going over the whole decision with him. A part of your prayer can include the important fact that even though you're excited, and even though you feel that this could be a good step for you, you are committed to his will and trust his understanding more than your own. In other words, submit yourself to God's purpose but don't feel any restriction from telling him your desire."

The more Wina and I talked, the more clear it became that she felt she had to make an appointment with God. She seemed to feel she needed to sit down, as though in a job interview, and say all the right words in just the right way or God would not hear her.

We need to be careful because prayer can become a very mechanical experience. Jesus warned us not to allow prayer to become "meaningless repetition." He knew how easy it is for humans to get superstitious and to think that repeating the "right" words over and over again would somehow buy time with God. It is true that sometimes we might spend a long time in prayer with God over a particular issue, and that we will have recurring discussions with him about subjects that are of importance to us, but that is not the same as just robotically going through the same routine over and over again.

It turned out that Wina, the woman who was praying for a job, was struggling with that kind of question about the prayer. "I try to imagine that he is interested in what I have to say, but I feel like I'm taking too much of his time, and I worry that I'm not doing it the way he wants."

"I realize that not everyone has had a good relationship with an earthly father," I replied, "but it is easier to understand our relationship with our heavenly Father if we compare it to a relationship we can visualize.

"Let's say you are a child, and your father is wise and caring and loves you very much," I continued. "One of the ways you know that is because of what he does for you. If you have a deep need or a deep desire, it will be natural for you to have numerous conversations with him about it. Let's suppose, for example, that you have become excited about horses. That's all you can think about. You will let your father know in the most effective terms possible, and as often as possible, how much you love horses and how badly you would like to have one. There may be times when you will talk with him about them several times a day.

"Your father may actually decide to buy you a horse. On the other hand, as an older person who knows more about life than you do, he might not be able to buy you one just yet because he feels that you're not ready or because there is some practical limitation, but because of his love he would never condemn you for having the desire."

"Yes, I guess that's true," she said.

"So, you see, a whole bunch of things are going on at once," I explained. "Your passion, your expression of that passion to your father on a frequent basis, your uncertainty about what might be decided, and your confidence that whatever the decision, nothing will mean that your father doesn't love you.

"In that scenario, your repeated conversations with your father would be because of your hunger to talk with your dad and to let him know what you want and how badly you want it. All of that would occur within your confidence of his love and his wish to see good things in your life."

"Okay, I'm seeing that," Wina said.

"Contrast that with another scene," I continued. "In this case, you approach your father with a previously learned formula in mind. Perhaps you stand outside his door, chanting your request, or you send him your requests in writing. All of it is done with the feeling that somehow you are buying his favor and accumulating assets that you can trade in for what you desire. Naturally, the more you chant or the more notes you write, the more currency you will have.

"It's as though you view God as a force, like electricity, that operates according to formulas, instead of being a personal Father. Or he's some kind of a slot machine so the more quarters you put in the better. Additionally, there is the suggestion that maybe Father doesn't really love me, and I have to earn everything that comes from him."

"That's what I've been feeling," she agreed. "I guess I'll have to work on that."

"I love a poster that somebody sent to me several years ago, Wina," I concluded. "It says IF YOU'RE HAVING TROUBLE WITH PRAYER . . . TALK TO GOD ABOUT IT."

Prayer is, essentially, spending time with God and talking with him. No particular form is required, as I told Wina, and prayer should not become a meaningless ritual. We don't need to be on our knees, our hands are not required to be folded, and, in fact, the Bible doesn't even say that we have to close our eyes. Nothing's wrong with those postures if they are important to you, but contrary to popular understanding, the Bible does not expect them.

Prayer is one of the most important sources of spiritual nourishment. It is being in God's presence, not only talking to him but hearing from him, having his influence on our lives and our considerations. Some people like to choose regular times of the day, such as the morning or night. Others choose variable times during the day or during the week.

It is important to be reminded, however, that prayer can occur at any time and in any place. The apostle Paul even encourages us to "pray without ceasing." In other words, there is never a time that from deep within there cannot be a heart of prayer to God. For many busy city dwellers, the car has become a sanctuary of prayer and spending time with God!

There's another aspect of prayer that is actually a part of nourishing other people. To illustrate it, imagine that a friend, for some reason, feels he is not able to talk with Father or has lost the confidence that he even wants to hear from him. In that case, we may go talk to Father on that person's behalf. That's called intercessory prayer. When we are carrying the needs and the burdens of other people into our time with God, we are actually participating in some of what can happen and is happening in that person's life.

The Nourishment of the Bible

God has always provided some written record of what he has said and done. In Chapter 10, I've described the fact that the Bible can serve as a measuring stick for those who want to make spiritually nourishing choices. It's more than that, however. It's God speaking to us. The Bible is a banquet table for the spiritually hungry heart, and we live in a time when virtually anybody can partake of it.

I think most of us recognize the value of reading and studying the Bible. I am sensitive about the fact, however, that many of those who respect the Bible are not nourished by reading it.

The importance of measuring our relationship with the Bible on the basis of nourishment is illustrated by a conversation I had with a woman whom I will call Georgia. "I know it's important to read the Bible," she complained. "But I just can't do it. I try, but I get bored or I get impatient. Sometimes I even fall asleep! I feel awful about it, and I know God must be disappointed in me. I hear about all these people in my church who read the Bible every day or who study the Bible, and I feel terribly guilty. Can you help me develop more of a desire to read the Bible? I really have to confess that I don't enjoy it."

I asked Georgia several questions to help me get a better picture of what she was going through. For one thing, it was clear that in her particular church you were not considered a part of the "in crowd" if you were not having some kind of a daily ritual with the Bible. I'm not criticizing that kind of daily feeding on the Word of God, but it can become a relic of legalism if we're not careful, and that's not nourishing!

Another factor occurred to me, however, which I pursued with Georgia. "Is it possible that you are the kind of person who does not read very much at all?" I asked. "Do you read other books?"

"No," Georgia answered quickly. "I've never been very good at reading."

"So a part of your difficulty with the Bible may have nothing to do with a lack of desire to read it," I suggested.

"You don't have a very good relationship with any reading materials."

"I've never thought about it that way," she said, "but that's right. I'm not a reader."

"That's an important ingredient in this discussion," I commented. "How'd you do in school?"

"Terrible!" she replied. "I was never a very good student."

"Have you ever been evaluated for a learning disability?" I asked.

"I don't think so," she answered.

I spent a few minutes describing some of the common evidences of a learning hindrance, including the fact that otherwise intelligent people often have trouble relating to pieces of paper. They're smart; they just can't read.

"I've always felt dumb," Georgia said with emotion in her voice. "I've worked harder than any other member of my family to try to succeed in school, but I've never been able to do it. I barely made it through high school."

I gave Georgia the telephone number of a professional who evaluates learning disorders, and I also gave her a suggestion. "You might try getting the Bible on cassette. I know several people with learning disorders who get a lot of nourishment from the Bible by listening to it on tape. For some, it has made all the difference in the world."

Several weeks later, I got a follow-up call from Georgia. "Guess what?" she said with gladness. "I'm not dumb! I do have a learning disability, and it is something that can be corrected through therapy so I've already started. I am amazed at how much I've already improved. Also, I did get the Bible on cassette, and I love it. I'm enjoying the Bible like I never have."

The point, I think, is clear. Our goal is to make spiritual choices that are going to result in nourishment and growth in our lives, not just a commitment to a procedure.

The "Shoulds" and "Oughts" Also Damage Our Study

I recently heard a radio teacher say that if you were not spending time in Bible Study every day, preferably at the same time each day, you cannot live like Christ. I wonder what his message would have been to Christians a thousand years ago, especially the ones who didn't know how to read. His point that we are richly nourished, spiritually and otherwise, by partaking of the Word of God is well taken.

Multitudes of people read the Bible out of guilt or even superstition. For some, daily Bible reading has become a good luck measure. They think, *If I read the Bible this morning, I may disarm any curses lurking around me that are designed to make my life miserable.*

I've run into this numerous times during my ministry, but one call to my radio program comes to mind from a person called Peter.

The Man Who Saw Bible Reading as a Ritual

Peter was deeply discouraged because he had been turned down for a job that he wanted badly. "I've been moping around the house for a week, trying to get over this," he told me. "I just don't understand what God is doing in my life. I've gone through school; I've been looking for the right job for more than a year. This job was perfect for what I wanted and needed, and I was sure I was going to get it. I can't comprehend why I didn't."

Nobody needs to apologize for feeling let down about something like that, but as I talked with Peter, it became clear to me that a mist of superstition surrounded his disappointment. He had the feeling that it was his turn "to be blessed," and that he had performed all the right rituals to be eligible for getting the job. That was especially apparent when he said, "I even stayed up most of the night before the interview reading the Bible."

"What portions did you read?"

"I don't really remember."

As we talked further, it became even clearer that Peter's nocturnal meandering through the Bible had not been nourishing to him at all but had been a ceremony that he felt would improve his chances of getting the job. I couldn't help but wonder if the poor guy had lost the job because he was so sleepy from performing that late-night ritual.

Different Ways of Reading the Bible Try to experiment and discover what will be nourishing in God's Word. To ignore the Bible or to go for long periods of time without partaking of it, I think we would all agree, is to miss out on essential nourishment.

Different people will choose different ways of being nourished from the Bible, and those ways may even change from time to time down the pathway of life. Some people read the Bible every day as a form of daily spiritual nourishment. Others study specific topics, like love or courage, in the Bible once or several times a month, receiving nourishment for particular hungers. Others choose to attend a Bible study where a teacher can help them understand the Scripture better.

The Bible doesn't designate any particular method of reading or studying, and, in fact, the Bible has only been available to people like you and me since the invention of the printing press. The goal is, however, to truly be nourished by God's Word and to use it as a measuring stick for much of what we believe.

Partaking of the Bible is not supposed to be a requirement that feels like kissing your least favorite cousin. It is to be a time of addressing your spiritual (and often your emotional) hunger, of gaining understanding, of maturing.

If the Bible is new to you, by the way, or you feel like you don't know your way around, there are several ways to begin. A great start is the book of John. It is near the beginning of the second half of the Bible, the New Testament, right after Matthew, Mark, and Luke. The book was written by one of Jesus' closest friends and disciples, so it provides a firsthand account of some of what Jesus did and said.

Some people like to read a little of the Bible each day. Your local Christian bookstore could probably provide a recommended list of scriptures for each day so you would read through the entire Bible in one year. There are also some special Bibles specifically designed for daily reading which provide a portion from the Old Testatment, a portion from the New Testament, and a portion from Psalms or Proverbs for each day of the year.

The Nourishment of Fellowship

Fellowship is, essentially, having a relationship with other followers of Christ. It is one of the forms of nourishment that God has designed for our needs. We can't grow by ourselves.

That's a vital point because many of us, especially if we are deeply hurting, tend to isolate ourselves. Even if we seem to be very social, we can sometimes be tremendously lonely inside. It's like a starving person going to a feast but pretending not to be hungry. All the ingredients for nourishment are there, but that person is not allowing himself to partake of them.

We need to have a "family" relationship with other Christians, preferably in a way that we can be open and honest about what is going on inside us. There is nourishment from being encouraged and held up by others when we are weak, from feedback from people whom we trust and who will be honest with us. There is nourishment from being together for prayer or feeding on God's Word or serving the needs of others.

One of the activities I enjoy most is fishing. It's not only nourishing to me to get away from the routine and to experience nature, but I also enjoy the friendship and the fellowship that can be a part of a trip like that.

On one of our summer trips to the Yukon, a man came along. I'll call him Carl. He wasn't much of a fisherman but a good friend of his had invited him because he felt Carl needed it.

There were six on the trip, including Carl. All were followers of Christ. In addition to all the fun and the scenery and the fishing and the food and the flying in floatplanes and the wildlife, we had a nourishingly good time spiritually. Sometimes we'd pair off and fish together in the small outboard boats and spend the entire day talking. Other times we met together around the dinner table or late at night around a campfire and talked openly and honestly about our lives. We had prayer together. Sometimes we sang to the Lord. Our entire week was punctuated with praise to God for the beauty and all that he had created.

On the final night of our trip, we were all packed and ready to leave the next morning. We gathered in the main room of the lodge where we were staying and reflected on the week and various things that had meant a lot to us. One of the first to speak was Carl. "I've been going through a tough time this year," he began. "Business has been slow, and it's taken a lot of time and effort on my part to keep things alive. That, combined with the demands of a family, has really drained me.

"My wife has been trying to tell me I need to plug into some Christian fellowship or to even become more of a part of the men's group at church. For some reason, that did not seem like a priority to me. I was so busy and so weighed down, that just seemed like another thing to do, and I didn't need the complication in my schedule.

"Then I was invited on this trip," Carl continued. "I don't fish very much, but I thought maybe the time away from the business would do me good so I decided to come." Carl's eyes moistened as he said, "I want you guys to know that I have never been so enriched by anything in all my life. Hearing you guys talk about your own struggles and hearing how much the Lord means in your lives has, I think, changed me. I feel more spiritually refreshed right now than I have in years, and I'm kicking myself for not drawing from this kind of strength before now. I just want to thank each of you."

Carl had not only experienced the nourishment of getting away from the pressures at home, but also the nourishment of spending time with other followers of Christ. I have seen Carl a couple of times since then, and he always comments on how much that week contributed to a change in his life.

Fellowship can mean a lot when we're hurting, but it's not only for suffering people. It is a regular part of the nourishment of the spiritual life. I believe God has designed things that way. None of us is meant to live life alone. None of us is able to totally experience what Christ offers without being with others who believe in him and follow him as well.

The Nourishment of Church

For most of us, the nourishment of fellowship will occur through relationship with a church. Church is a family of Christ followers.

A good church is meant to be a center for nourishment of all kinds. In addition to fellowship there is nourishment from the teaching of the Bible, the nourishment of prayer, the nourishment of worshiping God and giving to him, the nourishment of being helped by others or participating in helping others, and the nourishment of having respected leaders influence our lives.

A church can be a large, time honored place in the center of a city or it can be a small group of people who are meeting in someone's home. It can be a setting that is very formal and traditional or informal and non-traditional. Whatever the style or the setting, the church needs to be a place of nourishment.

A Church That Forgot about Nourishment   I have the privilege of speaking in a lot of different kinds of churches around the country. Unfortunately some of them stopped nourishing their members a long time ago. I was invited to a church in southern California several months ago that, from my perspective, was an example of what I am talking about.

Before I ever got to the church, I wondered if there was any nourishment there. The woman who communicated with me to make arrangements came across cold and mechanical. Even when I tried to explore some of what was happening at their church so I would have more of an idea of what to say when I spoke, it was as though I was talking to a foreigner. She had no idea what the church stood for, what was being experienced right now by the people at the church, or what might be of value to them. I dismissed the conversation as being representative of the woman only, but when I got to the church, I discovered otherwise.

I spent about twenty minutes with the pastor before we went into the sanctuary for the morning service. For most of our time together he talked about his members as though they were uncooperative employees. It was clear to me that he was not happy in the ministry. But he had pastored this church for many years, and there didn't seem to be any change in sight.

"People are just not committed to church anymore," he complained. "I have a dickens of a time getting these folks to attend a Sunday evening service. They're more interested in TV or baseball," he said sarcastically. "When I was a kid, we all came out for a Sunday evening service."

Later, during the morning service, I saw the pastor in action. He laid a guilt trip on that congregation that was spread as thick as peanut butter and stuck in everyone's throat about the same way. There was going to be a "work" day at the church on the following Saturday, for example, and he gave the impression that if the people didn't consider helping, they were just not good church members.

The whole spirit of the service was one of guilt and obligation. Because of that, the service was not nourishing for the congregation. I found myself wondering, *Why is this man pastoring when he is so obviously tormented by it? Why are these people here when they don't seem to be nourished by the experience?*

I wanted to say, "Pastor, have you thought about whether your service and activities are really spiritually nourishing? Is what you are doing appealing to those who are hungry? Is this really a place to feed souls or just an enterprise led by people who feel they 'should' keep it alive by trying to convince others that they 'should' participate because nobody would feel good if it died, especially since all the 'shoulds' seem to be coming from God—or at least from his representatives?"

Is Spiritual Food Really Being Served? Let me say, by the way, that the central issue in a church is one of what is being served and not necessarily the way it is being served. In other words, there are a lot of different kinds of churches: formal and informal, new and old, large and small, affiliated and non-affiliated, educated and not so educated, traditional and non-traditional. Some people who have left a formal church, which was not nourishing, to attend an informal church, which was nourishing, have come to think that the primary difference was the way the food was being served. Not so!

A lot of people have had the opposite experience. They have left an informal church, which was not nourishing, and found a formal one that was. I do think it is easier for an older, formal church to degenerate into something lifeless than a newer, less traditional church, which might have been formed recently by hungry people. However, non-traditional churches can become lifeless too. The difference is not only how spiritual food is being served, but whether it is being served.

In addition, we need to ask ourselves what kind of nourishment is going on. Sometimes churches lose vital spiritual nourishment because they replace it with other kinds of nourishment. That's how a church turns into a social club or a lecture hall or a concert hall.

Ministry is a matter of nourishment. If you're in the middle of a famine, all you have to do is set up a simple banquet with real food, and you'll be overwhelmed with people. If, however, the people you want to come to your banquet are not hungry or if the food you are serving is not real, the banquet becomes something else.

Imagine an organization, for example, which came into being during a severe famine and became famous for the large crowds that attended its banquets. Over time, however, fewer and fewer people attended the banquets, and the hosts began to wonder if the organization could survive. At that point the hosts need to conduct a sober self-evaluation to determine if the guests have stopped coming because the quality of the food has diminished or because the people are ignoring their hunger. In either case, it is easy for the leaders to think, *The sign of a good banquet is having a lot of people so let's do whatever we can to get people there*.

Pretty soon you've got "banquets" where the food is only incidental, and the real reason people are coming is because you have booked a traveling side show and are appealing to the people's hunger for entertainment. That which used to satisfy the spiritual hunger of starving people has become a tourist attraction.

Don't get me wrong. There is nothing wrong with having a stirring song at a banquet or a speaker who makes people laugh or stimulates the intellect. There is nothing automatically wrong with a well-planned extravaganza or an event that attracts public interest. There isn't anything wrong either if the people get together for recreation or entertainment after a good banquet. But a lot is wrong when spiritual nourishment has been replaced by those things.

· · · · · · · · ·

The Physical, Emotional, and Spiritual Become One

Let me re-emphasize this does not mean that spiritual nourishment is the only important nourishment. Remember that God is the one who created us as physical, emotional, and spiritual beings. Just because those are distinct parts of who we are, doesn't mean that we should isolate and give attention to only one of them. All our parts add up to make the whole. They interact and interrelate and should not be artificially separated. It is godly to eat a balanced meal. It is godly to be intellectually stimulated. It is godly to have fun. It is godly to pursue certain professional goals. It is godly to enjoy friendship.

There have been times in the history of faith when people have de-emphasized physical and emotional nourishment and have been preoccupied with what they considered to be spiritual nourishment. They have lived very confined lives, sometimes to the extent of imprisoning themselves in caves or small communities. They have rejected the world of colors and tastes and sensations and have cut themselves off from fun and discovery. In my mind, this type of life is a repudiation of some of the very things that God has given to us.

Some religious people have had an attitude that seems to say, "Yes, we can enjoy the world of colors, but not too much. Yes, we can enjoy physical nourishment, but don't make it taste too good." I remember hearing a pastor on a Christian television program criticize a certain sexual technique, not because he thought it was immoral, but because, in his view, it provided "too much pleasure."

We can get out of balance and become obsessed with

almost anything, including religious activity. Therefore, it is important to keep in mind that God has purposefully made us multidimensional and that paying attention to healthy nourishment for all of these dimensions is important to us and to him.

Ideally, for the Christian there is no artificial separation between physical, emotional, and spiritual. Every physical experience can be a part of an acknowledgment and praise of what God has created and provided. Every emotional experience can include God's presence and his leading or his comfort. Every spiritual act can and should be something from him or for him.

CHAPTER 12

· · · · · · · · · · · · ·

New Choices

Even after thinking about nourishment and being encouraged to be a more nourished person and to contemplate more effective ways of nourishing others, it is easy not to do it. It is safer for many of us to live in the world as we have always known it.

I want to be a voice that says, "Launch out!"

One of the most exciting aspects of nourishment is discovery.

Recently I cooked a meal for our family which included a bread stuffing dish. After the plates had been passed and we were all digging in, my eleven-year-old son, Kevin, held up a forkful of the stuffing and exclaimed, "What is this? It's delicious!"

"It's stuffing," I replied. "I decided to serve stuffing tonight instead of potatoes."

Kevin's expression changed suddenly, his chewing became a little less enthusiastic, and he said, "I've never liked stuffing before."

I guess his only experience with stuffing had been seeing it bulging from a Thanksgiving turkey, and the sight of it didn't appeal to him. If I had told him ahead of time what our "new dish" was called, he might not have tried it. But he did, and he was surprised and delighted by a new discovery.

We've all gone through that kind of experience—the discovery that something we thought we didn't like the taste of when we were young has become, to our older palates, a cherished delicacy. Or, we're finally persuaded to sample something we have never eaten before and find the flavor so wonderful we wish we had been eating it all our lives.

These experiences are steps of discovery, the recognition that nourishment as we have known it is not the only kind there is.

· · · · · · · · ·
Nourishment Inventory

As you embark on a new season of recognizing and discovering emotional and spiritual nourishment, I encourage you to take a "nourishment inventory." Sit down with a notebook or a piece of paper and list the various ways your life has been nourished in the past and the ways you are being nourished right now. Do you have the nourishment of friends and of family? Do you have a job or career or career goal that is nourishing to you and to others? What about your hobbies or personal interests? Music? Physical exercise? Nutrition? Rest or relaxation or recreation? Are you receiving spiritual nourishment?

Spend some time making your list and evaluating what you find. For some of us, there will be the realization that it has been days or weeks or even months since any significant nourishing has occurred. For others, there will be the recognition that what we've always considered to be nourishment may actually be an anemic substitute or may even be an addiction. Some of us will find there are only one or two sources of nourishment in our lives.

Another list you will want to make is one that summarizes the ways you offer nourishment to those around you, such as family or friends. You might even want to make specific lists for specific people. Some of the questions to ask yourself are: How do I offer nourishment to my wife (or husband)? Does she (he) consider it really nourishing? How do I nourish my child? How am I a source of nourishment to my friend? How can I participate in healthy nourishment with my mom or dad?

A third list might be the actual steps you can take toward better nourishment. Remember, being a nourished person is the result of walking a pathway of nourishment and making choices which lead in that direction. If you're not satisfied with your job or career, for example, a good first step might be to think of three or four people you feel are being fulfilled in their jobs and talk with them individually about what they recommend as the next step for you. Go ahead and make a telephone call to the college or training school you have always been curious about. Go ahead and contact the places where you have dreamed of working. Find out what the next choice can be. Or, if you're feeling inadequate as a husband or wife or parent, the next step may be to look for a book that will address that need or to arrange to have breakfast with a couple of other friends who are struggling with the same questions.

Don't just sit on the pathway of life watching other people walk by, wishing you could look like them.

Step onto the pathway.

You can't wait until you look and feel fully nourished. All you have to do is walk onto the path as the first step in making new choices. As you face the challenge of each next step, use The Nourishment Factor to measure when to take a step and in which direction.

Consider your own nourishment and the nourishment of

those around you. Define and protect the boundaries that
will keep you healthy. Respect the boundaries of others.

Take God's hand as you walk on the pathway of life and,
above all, be nourished by him.

May you be good to yourself and to those around you.
That is my prayer.

About the Author

Rich Buhler is host of the nationally syndicated radio program, "TableTalk," which is broadcast daily from Los Angeles. For nearly ten years, he was host of the pioneering talk show, "Talk from the Heart," in southern California.

Buhler has more than twenty years of ministry and broadcast experience including positions with Westinghouse Broadcasting and CBS News.

He is the host of two award-winning films, *Fractured Families* and *They Lied to Us*. His previous books include *Love: No Strings Attached*, and *Pain and Pretending*.